To Pat & Vince who were
part of our adventure
in Chapter 14.

Best —

Barbara

NO SUBSTITUTE FOR QUALITY

The Many Worlds of
Lawrence A. Fleischman

No Substitute For Quality

The Many Worlds of
Lawrence A. Fleischman

BY BARBARA G. FLEISCHMAN

GREENWICH PUBLISHING GROUP, INC.
LYME, CONNECTICUT

Produced and published by Greenwich Publishing Group, Inc., Lyme, Connecticut

Design by Tom Goddard Design
Higganum, Connecticut

Library of Congress Catalog Card Number: 94-74466

ISBN: 0-944641-08-3

First Printing: February 1995

CONTENTS

ACKNOWLEDGEMENTS

Several years ago while traveling in Europe with our good friends Bob and Clarice Smith, during a leisurely luncheon, Larry was regaling them with one of his adventures. They turned to me and said, "You should write a book about Larry!" And so I have — and I thank them for giving me the idea.

I want to thank all my children for their enthusiastic support and encouragement when I told them of this project. However, this mission simply could not have been accomplished without the patience and ongoing hand-holding of my daughter, Martha. She first introduced me to my new friend and sometimes nemesis, the word processor, and helped me to work with it, calming my frustrations on an almost daily basis. Finally, she helped jog my memory with her fine editing. Without her I simply could not have done the job.

Special thanks go to my friend Nancy Sureck who, out of friendship, offered to lend her great editing skills to me which she did with such generosity.

And, finally, to Larry himself who has often expressed the fact that our life together has been a series of exciting chapters — he has not only been a great life partner but a fascinating full-length book!

DEDICATION

To Larry, of course,
with pride, respect and
all my love on
the occasion of his
70th birthday

CHAPTER 1

A Meeting

ON JUNE 9, 1947, A MEETING WAS CALLED FOR THE NEW BOARD OF THE Junior Division of the Allied Campaign in Detroit. The agenda was to discuss the enormous pressure to get all the remaining Jews out of Europe who wished to emigrate to Israel and elsewhere. For the first time, a young adult group of potential leaders had come to the fore.

Among them was a "hot shot" volunteer that I heard had just returned from the Army and had not only given his mustering-out pay to the campaign but had already solicited about a hundred prospects. Following the board meeting, a group of us repaired to a local ice cream parlor, and I was introduced to Larry Fleischman, an attractive, articulate and dedicated 22-year-old fellow from whom one could detect, in addition to charm, an obvious sign of leadership. He was olive-skinned, slim and bespectacled, with dark brown curly hair and a self-confident tilt to his head that was very compelling to me.

I apparently failed the first test by not ordering a chocolate milk shake. Chocolate milk shakes were and still are a passion of Larry's and have continued as one of the leitmotifs of our courtship and indeed our more than 46 years together.

We got off to a worse start when after the introduction I asked this brash young man what he did. He shot back, "Do you mean to tell me that you haven't heard of the Arthur Fleischman Carpet Company?"

My immediate rejoinder was, "Isn't that the company which is long overdue in delivering my parents' new carpeting?"

Firmly he stated, "There's no substitute for quality and that's why you've had to wait — we're giving you the best quality of carpets!" This, then, was my introduction to Lawrence A. Fleischman and the beginning of our life-long romance.

This phrase "no substitute for quality" has echoed over the years ever since, first in regard to floor covering, then the world of art and finally every aspect of our life.

My new acquaintance was born on the east side of Detroit, Michigan, on February 14, 1925, the son of Stella Granet Fleischman and Arthur Fleischman, émigrés from Russia — she from near Odessa and he from the area of Minsk

Arthur was a squarely built and muscular man with a strong and slightly Slavic cast to his face. Having arrived in the United States with virtually no money, he began his business career by renting a horse and buggy and selling oilcloth and other household notions to local Michigan farmers — often sleeping under the trees next to his wagon.

Stella, a small and shy woman with great sensitivity and love of beauty, met and married Arthur in 1923. They worked side by side with Stella sewing window shades and Arthur selling linoleum and then carpets. After meeting Larry's parents, it became obvious to me that he inherited his drive and strong personality from his father and his sensitivity and passion for beautiful things from his mother.

Following Larry's birth in 1925, the Fleischman family was completed in 1930 by the arrival of another son, Irving. The family then lived comfortably in a large flat above the carpet store on Gratiot Avenue on the east side of Detroit. The neighborhood was largely made up of German-American families and as Larry grew up, it became apparent that the local schools were not giving this bright boy a challenging enough education.

The family was prospering financially, primarily as a result of the grinding, seven-day work week both parents maintained. Larry was left to fend for himself and take care of his younger brother. Some of his happiest activities were playing in the store, making crates out of the spare wood around the installation department and attending the local movie theater, where on Saturdays he could see a double-feature, a serial and be given a free tap-dancing lesson — all for just ten cents.

As he approached his 13th birthday, Larry began instruction for his impending Bar Mitzvah. He also studied fencing, an activity that gave him great pleasure, with the great fencer and renowned teacher Bela deTuscan.

As the war in Europe began to loom in local consciousness, a markedly pro-German attitude began to be noticeable in the neighborhood. There was an open allegiance on the part of many neighbors to the local German-American Bund. This reinforced the determination of the senior Fleischmans to find a better school for Larry. Through the recommendation of friends they arranged to send him to Western Military Academy in Alton, Illinois, and in 1938, he was enrolled in the ninth grade.

Although the idea of a military academy was not truly in keeping with Larry's attitudes, he always credited it with instilling certain disciplines and study habits in him and giving him an excellent high school education along with an emphasis on good manners.

While at the academy, he was exposed to two influences that have had a lifelong effect upon him. First, his roommate's father was on the board of the St. Louis Opera Company and thus, the two boys were frequently invited to attend a performance. This experience gave Larry an enjoyment of grand opera that has lasted to this day. A chance meeting with Jeanette MacDonald, who was performing in one of the operas, left him with a permanent soft spot in his heart for the auburn-trussed singer and movie star.

It was also at this time that he developed a keen interest in photography. Nourishing a burgeoning entrepreneurial spirit, he began photographing his fellow cadets in uniform. Apparently, the business met with such success that the enterprising young cadet was called in by Major Persing, the head of the school, who suggested that a fuller concentration on academics for Larry would be in everyone's best interest. The business was thus terminated. However, Larry's fascination with photography persisted and gave him the insights, skills and interest that ultimately led to a passion for art that has continued to expand throughout his life.

He graduated from Western Military Academy in 1941 at the age of 16. Although he yearned to enter Massachusetts Institute of Technology, his parents had decided he was too young for that institution. Instead, he entered Purdue University as an engineering student.

It should be noted that his parents, his father particularly, practiced the European or old-school tradition in which children were not praised for fear of "spoiling" them. Children were to follow the wisdom and dictates of their parents, and overt signs of affection towards children were not appropriate. In that atmosphere, he acquiesced to the decision to attend Purdue University's engineering school.

His enjoyment of university life and participation in fraternity activities at Tau Beta Phi was profoundly shaken by a personal tragedy. His beloved younger brother, Irving, died suddenly at the age of 11 of an embolism following elective surgery on a deviated septum. Instead of welcoming his brother to a Purdue football weekend as planned, Larry sped home to Detroit to comfort his parents and attend the funeral.

His mother, who especially doted upon her younger son, was devastated and was on the verge of a nervous breakdown; his father closed himself in to deal with his grief. They both apparently had a misplaced sense of guilt because the child had not wanted the operation. Sadly, no attention was paid to Larry's loss, so at this emotional time, once again, he had to fend for himself and face his grief alone.

He returned to Purdue and continued his studies as the United States entered World War II. As the war intensified and students and friends all around him were entering the armed services in one way or another, Larry decided to apply for the A.S.T.P (Army Specialized Training Program) which trained young students for the military and then returned them to college campuses to complete their educations.

The spirit of those times was strong — the United States had embarked upon a mission to right terrible wrongs, to defeat

Adolf Hitler, his cohorts and the Japanese and to "make a better world for the future."

Larry's father, having emigrated from the tyrannical world of Czarist Russia, had become a passionate American. His son was imbued with that same love of his country and was dedicated to join it in its hour of need.

Because Larry's eyesight was not good, he memorized the eye chart, passed the physical examination and entered the U.S. Army in the fall of 1943. After weeks of basic and other training at Fort Benning, Georgia, the young soldier and some of his buddies were loaded on a train headed to Washington University in St. Louis, Missouri, to complete their college education. The following morning as he lifted the window shade, he peered out at what turned out to be Camp McKain, Mississippi.

As they soon learned, due to the increased ferocity of the war and the consequent need for freshly trained troops, the A.S.T.P. had been canceled, and all the college men were put into infantry training. Not for the first time in Larry's active army career, an army doctor examining him at a new assignment asked, "What the devil are you doing in the army with such bad eyesight? You'd better always have an extra pair of glasses!"

So, in the summer of 1944, an odd mixture of young college boys and Southern hillbillies who had never left home before were shipped to Europe in five days on the *Queen Elizabeth*.

One of his first very moving human experiences was that of living with young men serving in the Army who could not read or write to their loved ones. Larry wrote many letters home for his illiterate new friends. This experience also opened up another avenue for mutual understanding, as many of these men had never before met anyone Jewish. Through their acquaintance with Larry, they began to realize that Jews were not strange and different creatures, and Larry never felt a whiff of anti-Semitism.

In August, D-Day plus 60, their regiment of the 94th Infantry Division of the Third Army landed on Omaha Beach. After several months of combat and battles, Larry was slightly wounded in St. Nazaire, France, and briefly hospitalized.

Their company had been repeatedly told not to enter the numerous deserted houses in case they were mined, as often was the case. Sure enough, one of his buddies set out to see if there was anything of interest as a souvenir in one of the houses. Larry went after him, pulling him out just as an explosion blew them both through the air.

Swiftly recovering from a knee injury, Sergeant Fleischman was sent to Grave Registration School in Besanscon where their group's main task was to scout the areas of Normandy and Brittany where American planes had been downed or crashed. Their task was to find what had happened to survivors and to find where the dead had been buried so they could be relocated to American military cemeteries.

A letter arrived at this point from his father asking if he could track down a French family that was in dire need. They were relatives of well-to-do friends of Larry's parents in Detroit. The husband of the family, a physicist, had been hiding in Paris with his wife and two tiny daughters. Being Jewish, the physicist realized that he was in danger but, after a while, was lulled into thinking it was safe. He went out to get a loaf of bread one day and was picked up, never to be heard from again.

The distraught young wife was ultimately spirited away into the countryside with her children. They were now not too far away from where Larry was stationed. Apparently, they had little to eat and were desperate

Larry personally told and re-told the story throughout his entire company. With typical American generosity, his friends donated money, cigarettes, chocolates and other items which could be used for bartering, Larry arranged to have them delivered to the family. The family survived with the help of these contributions and later, in an extraordinary way, turned up in our lives in Buenos Aires, Argentina — but that's another chapter.

During this period in Besanscon something happened that was to have a profound effect on Larry's future interests and life. In one of his off-duty periods he was wandering about the Roman ruins in that French town and encountered a local physician who struck up a conversation with the lonely soldier.

It turned out that this man was an ardent collector of art and, sensing Larry's incipient interest in the ancient world and works of art, befriended him, invited him to his home, introduced him to his family and showed him his paintings and works of art. The doctor's enthusiasm and passion for beautiful things and the joy of living with them made an enduring impression upon Larry.

Shortly thereafter, Larry was selected to participate in an experiment that the U.S. Army was launching. With the expectation that there would be a large occupying army left in Europe, the Army decided to open a school in which some of the G.I.s would study with outstanding professors recruited from major American universities in a variety of disciplines. Larry was sent to Shrivenham in England and for some months received the benefits of this project until the school was ultimately closed. Although the war had drawn to an end and Larry had enough points to go home, he was deemed still necessary to Grave Registration and was sent back to France.

Mothers, widows and other next-of-kin were trickling over to Europe to visit the graves of their loved ones. Larry became increasingly enraged at the lack of care at some of the military cemeteries where the crosses and stars of David needed fresh paint and the grounds looked unkempt.

The commanding officer seemingly concentrated more on high living, good cognac and beautiful women and paid little attention to the cemeteries. After protesting through channels and getting no response, with the approval of his colonel Sergeant Fleischman sent a letter to the Inspector General which we have in our "archives." The Inspector General speedily looked into the matter.

This brought about some immediate changes in the upkeep of the cemeteries and soon after, Larry was released to go home. The Liberty ship which returned Larry and many of his comrades to New York took three weeks to make the crossing. During the voyage he caught a glimpse of the officer responsible for the neglected graves but made sure that their paths didn't cross! Sighting the Statue of Liberty from the ship's prow as they steamed into New York harbor was an emotional

NO SUBSTITUTE FOR QUALITY

experience that Larry says he will never forget.

Returning to Detroit, the now-former G.I. had to make some concrete decisions about his future. His mother was still emotionally fragile after the death of her younger son, and Larry felt an obligation to be supportive; his father was eager for him to join the family business. Despite the fact that he would have liked to leave Detroit, finish his college career and carve out a life elsewhere, this family situation made him elect to stay home and enter the Jesuit University of Detroit

Larry moved back into the family apartment above the carpet store and embarked upon a life of carrying a full academic load in the Physics Department, selling floor covering and trying to rebuild a social and community life. That's when our memorable meeting in the soda shop took place and transformed both of our lives.

CHAPTER 2

Courtship

FROM THE MOMENT OF OUR MEETING IN JUNE 1947 UNTIL OUR engagement on August 22, 1948, our courtship had many of the overtones of a comic opera.

Since we were both very active in the Junior Service Group of the Allied Jewish Campaign (I as campaign co-chairman and Larry as special gifts chairman), we were thrown together constantly. We began to "date," going out with our other campaign friends but often "double-dated," each going out with another but in the same group.

Often one could see that Larry was torn between being attentive to his partner for the evening and still trying to impress me, a daunting task. To complicate matters further he would call me two or three times an evening after his classes or work.

From time to time, totally out of context, he would repeat to me the story of Andrew Carnegie and how like Carnegie, Larry didn't want to marry until he was at least in his thirties and had accomplished a great deal in his career. I learned many years later that, indeed, Carnegie was 52 when he was married. However, at that time Larry's unsolicited protestations amused me, and I said to myself, "Methinks the gentleman doth protest too much!"

At this time to get more visibility for the Junior Service Group, we decided to have a Chanukah Hop, a dance for the younger folks in the Jewish community who would buy tickets and start to get involved in our fund-raising efforts. It's hard to know why the event didn't appeal to the audience we were trying to target, but it didn't work out and was forever tagged the "Chanukah Flop" by the committee. Amazingly enough, through all the years of planning events with Larry for all types of causes, this "Chanukah Flop" was the only out-and-out failure!

My would-be suitor was working full time at the Arthur Fleischman Company and carrying a full load of classes at University of Detroit, when he began making the long trip from the east side of Detroit where he lived, to the northwest part of Detroit, where my home was. My father shook his head in wonderment at the energy and persistence of this young man.

He had also embarked on an imaginative project for the Junior Service Group, that of organizing a fund-raising dinner for the young adults which for the first time would charge $100 apiece! As a drawing card, he persuaded the powers-that-be at the Federation to bring to Detroit for our event (and for his first visit), Max Lerner, the well-known columnist and liberal spokesman.

Despite the objections on the part of some community leaders that Mr. Lerner was "pinko," Larry, with the help of some of the rest of our young leadership, produced an enormously successful dinner raising a substantial sum of money. It was amusing to note that thereafter the Federation continued to bring Mr. Lerner to Detroit for other fund-raising events.

Also at this time, the Detroit Symphony was in dire straits, due to the withdrawal of support from the largest donor, and the season had been canceled. Larry, together with others, had formed a committee to create the Little Symphony, the purpose of which was to raise enough money to keep the major classical musicians in Detroit and create a short season until major funding was restored.

Since many music lovers in Detroit were fearful that the most talented musicians would depart the city, the campaign for the Little Symphony had a special urgency. So, from time to time our dates would consist of calling on prospects and other concerned patrons. Incidentally, money was raised and the goal of keeping the talented musicians was attained.

As the vice president of the Arthur Fleischman Carpet Company Larry's main responsibility was selling, and from the beginning he was indeed a "crack" salesman. In the late forties, there was a boom in home furnishings as the returning G.I.s began to marry, buy and rent new homes which needed to be furnished. In addition to the retail department, the Fleischman Company had a large contract division which sold to corporations, city institutions and other organizations.

The senior Fleischmans had prospered and now had three stores along with a variety of real estate holdings including apartments, commercial buildings and an elegant apartment-hotel, the Lee Plaza. Despite Larry's seemingly important title of vice president, it was clear from the beginning that his father's natural instinct would always be to dominate. However, Larry was still young and hopeful that he would soon take his place as a leader in the business.

During the summer of 1948, at age 23, he finally abandoned all hope of following in Andrew Carnegie's advice. He told me that while crossing Detroit on the highway to pick up another young lady for a date he said to himself, "Why am I doing this — I only want to be with Barbara!" This, then, was the beginning of the end of his bachelorhood and we soon became engaged.

My swain brought me home to meet his parents at Sunday dinner at their apartment. It was a blazing hot day, but Mrs. Fleischman had outdone herself to produce an elaborate dinner with many side dishes. As I struggled to show my enthusiasm for her cuisine, it became apparent that the groom-to-be was eating nothing. When queried by his mother as to why this was the case, he responded by saying with some asperity, "You know I never eat in hot weather!" Needless to say, this was news to his mother, and throughout the years I have never witnessed this strange aberration again. It obviously was sheer nerves.

As we prepared to announce our engagement, Larry had said something to me which has resonated through all of our years together. He stated, "Barbara, I can't promise you that we'll ever be rich, but our life will not be dull!" This has proved to be a watchword for me in that we have been rich in the most important sense of the word — that is, in experiences, relationships and adventures — we certainly have never had a dull moment.

After a round of parties and celebrations that fall, we were married at a small but lovely wedding at the Book-Cadillac Hotel. Our honeymoon took us to Miami Beach, Havana and Chicago, after which we settled down temporarily in the family-owned Lee Plaza Hotel.

I continued to work at the Greenberg Insurance Agency (my father's company) where the staff was witness to an amusing phenomena, that of my new young husband sauntering casually into the office every Friday — on my payday.

And so our adventure together began.

MY BIRTHDAY ON MARCH 20, 1949, WAS TRULY A SIGNIFICANT OCCASION

CHAPTER 3

Introduction to American Art

because Larry had searched painstakingly for a special present for his new bride. He wandered into the fine arts department of our largest Detroit department store, the J.L. Hudson Company, and selected a small but handsome colored etching by an artist named Max Pollak. The print was named, *Mexico — The Bells of Trin Tran Trin*. It can truly be said that this simple purchase signaled the opening of a whole new dimension to our life and changed it forever. I loved the etching and cherish it to this day as it still hangs proudly in our home as a very important symbol of an important beginning.

Our research into the life and work of Max Pollak brought us very little in the way of hard facts. What we did glean was that this artist, although not Jewish, was anti-Nazi and so all of his plates were destroyed. He fled his native Germany and spent the rest of his life working in Mexico.

By this time, we had moved from the elegant Lee Plaza Hotel where, as members of the owning family, we were too visible. We welcomed the wonderful anonymity of a small three-room apartment in a modest building also owned by the family. We hung the etching in our new apartment, which we were slowly furnishing.

Larry and I began to study this charming work of art and developed a fascination for the very craft and process of print-making. So that October, celebrating Larry's recent graduation

NO SUBSTITUTE FOR QUALITY

from the University of Detroit, we embarked on our first trip as married folk to New York City, and meandered into Associated American Artists where a lovely gentleman named Robert Price introduced us to the world of the $5 fine print.

The Associated American Artists gallery had developed a special approach to collecting prints by commissioning well-known artists to produce an edition of a print (most usually 100) and selling them for $5 apiece. This obviously created a new market whereby people of modest means could be introduced to the world of original prints and also artists became assured of a steady income for their prints and visibility to a widening public.

We entered this world with great gusto and began buying prints by such artists as Joseph Hirsch, Mervin Jules, Thomas Hart Benton, etc. As the next year and a half rolled on, we timidly added a Joe Jones watercolor, a George Grosz drawing and a Picasso *Three Graces* print to our tiny collection. We were infected and "hooked" for good.

This period produced a much more important acquisition with the arrival in January 1950, of our first child, Rebecca Nan. Her anticipated arrival made clear to us that the apartment, while cozy for a twosome, would be a tight squeeze for this burgeoning family. We sold two lots that had been given to us by the senior Fleischmans as a wedding gift, and began to look for a house. We bought a new, handsome, New Orleans colonial house in the Palmer Woods section of northwest Detroit and moved in with our new baby a few months later. Although we didn't have much furniture for a time, we were able to create a warm atmosphere with our small group of prints.

At about the same time that I was giving birth to Rebecca, Larry had given birth to an imaginative idea. In the process of selling carpeting he had been struck by the boring limitations of the product. Carpeting came in a variety of textures but was primarily limited as to color to beige, gray, rose, and green or floral.

For the first of many times in our married life, but not the last, he "bounced" an idea off of me to get my reaction. "How would it be if the Arthur Fleischman Carpet Company

22

sponsored a national Carpet Design Competition to encourage artists, designers, decorators, etc., to bring new ideas to the fore and put more vitality into the patterns?" he asked.

The enthusiasm of my response encouraged him to take this notion to a new acquaintance, William E. Woolfenden, then the curator of the education department of the Detroit Institute of Arts. One of the great museums of the United States, the Institute had long enjoyed a special reputation for its support of local artists and craftsmen. Woolfenden had been in charge, particularly, of the bi-annual Michigan Crafts Show for which he had a special taste and affinity. Thus, it seemed logical to see if he would be interested in this competition.

He found it a fascinating idea, obtained the approval of Edgar P. "Ted" Richardson, the director of the museum and, with Larry, organized the project to take place in 1951. The Arthur Fleischman Company offered a prize of $1,000 to be divided among the top three winners and the announcement drew 1,200 entries from 47 states and from American students abroad.

The jury was a distinguished one including heads of Bigelow-Sanford Carpet Company and Alexander Smith & Sons Company; Adele Weibel, curator emeritus of textiles at the Detroit Institute of Arts; Messrs. Woolfenden and Richardson; Edith B. Crumb, home furnishings editor of the *Detroit News*; and Talmadge C. Hughes, executive director of the Michigan Society of Architects. A blue ribbon advisory committee from all over the state of Michigan was also appointed.

The winners were a gentleman from the Chicago Art Institute, a young lady who was studying textile design in Pennsylvania and a nun from Chicago.

Larry spoke at the Detroit Institute of Arts for the first time in March of 1951. The title of his talk was, "The Carpet Story," and the entire project received an enormous amount of press.

The American Federation of Art was so impressed with the exhibit that it arranged a tour through eight Michigan cities and then all across the United States. The response was so widespread that the way was paved for the next step — an expansion of the project through the creation of an International

Carpet Design Competition. This competition had even more far-reaching effects upon future designs in the carpet industry because this time Larry promised that the design of the first prize winner would be produced commercially.

During this period an even more important product entered our family with the birth of our son, Arthur, in October 1951.

In 1952 the announcement of the competition went worldwide, offering $2,100 in prizes from the Arthur Fleischman Company. It attracted designs from 848 artists in the United States and an equal number of entries from 43 foreign countries.

The distinguished jury, headed by Ted Richardson, included Charles Eames, the well-known designer; Hollis S. Baker, the president of the Baker Furniture Company; Frank Masland III of the Masland Carpet Company; Eero Saarinen, the architect; Belle Krasne, editor of *Art Digest*; and Charles Nagel, director of the Brooklyn Museum.

The winners were announced in February 1953, and the top 91 designs were exhibited at the Detroit Institute of Arts in March at a reception with an illustrious international patrons committee and appropriate fanfare. The first and second prizes were won by an artist from Vienna, the third prize by a Californian and the fourth prize by an artist from the Cranbrook Academy in Bloomfield Hills, Michigan. An interesting observation from the jury was that there appeared to be no difference between designs from the United States and those from the rest of the world.

There was an even greater amount of media attention paid to this competition and the exhibit toured several museums throughout the United States. The impact upon the industry which Larry had sought came to fruition, and it wasn't long before there were enormous changes in carpet design.

Several years later when we were deep into collecting American art and particularly fascinated with the work of Stuart Davis, Larry worked with the V'Soske Carpet Company, which had its plant in Puerto Rico, to produce a stunning area rug of a Stuart Davis design, named *The Flying Carpet*. These rugs were in a limited edition and so well accepted that they certainly paved the way for the future proliferation of accent rugs.

As a sidelight to the carpet design project, Larry had his first experience with the television industry, making a few appearances on local television, and even the *Dave Garroway Show*, an early talk show which was aired from Chicago.

Around that time Larry, and his father were persuaded that television advertising would be successful for the Arthur Fleischman Company. Larry's father, however, was convinced that Larry should be featured in the commercials to provide a graphic identification for the company. So, the company sponsored a weekly dramatic program and Larry, reluctantly, but with the assistance of a funny cartoon symbol called "Professor All-Wooley," did the live commercials. As a matter of fact, on the night of October 14, 1953, after giving the commercial, he sped from the television studio to the hospital where he welcomed the arrival of our second daughter, Martha.

These brushes with the television industry were a foreshadowing of a more direct association with television in the years ahead.

CHAPTER 4

Detroit Art Community

OUR INTEREST IN COLLECTING AMERICAN ART TOOK A BIG LEAP FORWARD with a trip to New York City in April 1952.

We had earlier been introduced to outstanding artists in Michigan such as painters Sarkis Sarkisian, Guy Palazzola, Constance Richardson and Hughie Lee-Smith, the sculptor Walter Midener, the incredible potter John Foster and Earl Krentzin, the imaginative sculptor in silver. We purchased some fine examples of their work. It was exciting for us to see that there were such talented artists in our own backyard.

In anticipation of our planned trip to New York, our new mentor, Ted Richardson, gave us a list of the finest galleries in the city dealing in American art. Being an outstanding scholar and author in that field, he was delighted at our enthusiasm for American art and was only too willing to encourage us and send us to the best sources.

On a balmy New York spring day we found ourselves on the premises of the Downtown Gallery, owned by the formidable and extraordinary Edith Halpert. This dynamic and charismatic white-haired woman, with her passionate commitment to American art, especially the artists she represented, was unaccountably taken with Larry whose newly found excitement for this field almost matched hers. Her toughness was matched by his, as was her tenacity.

We spent several hours with her looking at her stable of amazing artists. On the sidewalk outside her 51st Street gallery we found ourselves in a daze having purchased four new works of art! The "crack" salesman had truly met another great salesman! Now the question was — and it was a question that would recur often over the years — how on our modest income were we going to pay for this exciting interest?

We had enhanced our embryonic collection with a Raymond Breinin, a Yasuo Kunyioshi, a small Stuart Davis and a Ben Shahn. Our eyes had been opened to the entire mesmerizing world of the Downtown Gallery's group of painters including Jack Levine, John Marin and Arthur G. Dove.

At about the same time, also through the introduction of Ted Richardson, we had met the well-known international antiquarian, Dr. Jakob Hirsch, and had purchased several small works from the ancient world, including a bronze Roman lamp in the shape of an artichoke. Through Larry's fascination with ancient history, we now had one foot in the ancient world and the other in twentieth century American art.

Although we couldn't meet the amazing creators of art of antiquity, Edith Halpert, with her lively and famous dinner parties in her apartment above the gallery, introduced us to the Stuart Davises, the Ben Shahns, the Jack Levines, John Marin and a variety of fascinating people. Meeting these incredible artists led to invitations to visit their studios, which gave us added insights into the processes of creativity.

We had delightful visits with John Marin, a most articulate Yankee, and were thrilled to see the studio where he created such lively and brilliant works of art. Once, when we were driving to his home in New Jersey, he turned to Larry and queried, "Why did you marry Barbara?" After a moment Larry responded by saying, "Because she could bake a great lemon meringue pie." Larry then countered by asking Marin, "And why did you marry your wife?" With a chuckle the artist replied, "Because she was the only one who could cut my hair properly!"

Visiting Stuart Davis was exciting and also amusing when we encountered him painting with his radio blasting some great jazz. His first question to us in his gravely voice was, "Can you Detroiters tell me what's going on with the Detroit Lions?"

In short order our view of the New York art world was

27

expanded to encompass many other galleries, and in addition to becoming familiar with the work of Charles E. Burchfield and Edward Hopper, among others, we developed a curiosity for the artist painting earlier in the twentieth century and, indeed, back to the beginnings of the United States from the period of the Revolution on.

We were often in debt as a result of our headlong enthusiasm for acquiring works of art, and it was hard to explain this to others at a time when so few people were interested in American art. My parents, for example, tried to encourage us to buy one or two paintings a year but we explained that great things did not appear on the market in a orderly fashion so they eventually accepted our rather irrational and compulsive approach to collecting.

In November 1953, our small collection was borrowed by my alma mater, the University of Michigan, and for the first time we had the pleasure of sharing our collection with others. Larry's philosophy about collecting has always placed strong emphasis on sharing what we were doing not only with scholars and curators but anyone who had a serious interest in what we were collecting.

The reception at the University of Michigan Art Museum was lovely. We were excited by the occasion and have always remembered with a special chuckle our encounter with a woman and her nine-year-old little girl. The mother was praising our exhibit in an almost gushing way. Caught up in the praise, I looked down at her little girl and asked, "And what did you like the best?" to which she responded with great enthusiasm, "The cookies!" Despite her mother's obvious discomfort, we were delighted with the honest response which we've never forgotten — it puts things in proper perspective.

The Detroit Institute of Arts had long had a tradition of "Works in Progress" or "little shows" which highlighted the latest works of living American painters. These mini-exhibitions served important purposes, giving visibility to outstanding contemporary talent, encouraging practicing artists and awakening interest in the Detroit community. Due to the fact that we had been gathering a large collection of the works of

John Marin, the museum decided to expand what had been originally intended as a "little show" and created a beautiful exhibit of John Marin's work, to which we loaned a group of our paintings in 1954.

By that year our good friends and acquaintances in Detroit realized that Larry and I had embarked on an exciting adventure. Our interest seemed to be contagious, and many of them shared our enthusiasm. Larry had the happy idea to organize a study group so that a few of us could gather monthly in each others' homes and hear lectures on various aspects of American art. Thus, Art Adventurers was born. We invited nine other couples to join the embryonic group, and Larry began to serve as the one-man program committee with me as his assistant. Over the months ahead, we heard talks from Ted Richardson, Lloyd Goodrich (then the director of the Whitney Museum), the artist Abraham Rattner, and the New York collector of American art, Roy Neuberger. In short order, the Art Adventurers consisted of five groups and we found ourselves planning programs for them all. It was a daunting task but gratifying because 50 couples were able to learn more about American art.

In early 1955 Larry decided that he wanted a portrait painted of me and our three children. After much careful consultation with Ted Richardson, it was decided to offer the commission to the man Ted thought was the best portrait painter in the United States, the Philadelphia artist, Franklin Watkins. After examining a lot of his work, some of which was in the collection of the Detroit Institute of Arts, Larry called him and invited him to come out to meet with us, which he did.

When this tall, aquiline-faced, elegant and urbane man arrived on the train from Philadelphia, we were all immediately captivated by him. Franklin, known as "Watty," was immediately challenged by the commission but was so taken with Larry that he insisted that it be a complete family portrait. He also suggested that he would paint it as what is called a "conversation piece" — a group of portraits in a genre setting.

After all the arrangements were made, on a steamy July day in what was a particularly hot and humid Detroit summer, the Watkins station wagon, complete with Watty's beautiful and lively wife, Ida, and their large poodle, found its way to our fair city. The following nine weeks were a remarkable experience for us all. Our children of course were still young (Rebecca was five and a half, Arthur almost four, and Martha not quite two years old) and as Watty explained, it would be impossible to require them to "sit." He said it was like trying to pose birds on the wing. However, he set up a large easel and canvas in our living room, where it remained for the nine-week period, and proceeded to create this complex composition.

This adventure was special on many levels. The Watkins were warm, sophisticated and witty people and absolutely delightful to be with. In addition, Watty was an extraordinarily sensitive and articulate artist, so that conversational exchange was stimulating and profound. A deep and happy friendship emerged with them both.

For a man who had never had children of his own, he was entrancing to ours. They raced through the living room frequently calling out to the busy artist, "Watty, I'm posing, I'm posing!" but he was never daunted by these interruptions and took all three of them seriously and with charming patience.

It was fascinating to watch the composition change and evolve over the weeks and to observe just how difficult and painful the act of creation is for a dedicated painter. For example, as the summer heat persisted, the little sunsuit that Martha was wearing became a topless romper and the lawn outside the window in the painting showed signs of parching and burning.

Working as he did on a daily basis, Watty became an intimate part of our family life and became especially fond of our wonderful housekeeper, Georgia Smith. He was especially tickled when each morning her husband delivered her to our house in their swanky pink Cadillac. Watty loved to say, "This is what makes America so special!"

For Larry, the friendship with Watkins was a significant one. He could visit with this wise man often and learn more and more about what makes an outstanding artist tick. It was a real treat for him to go to the museum with Watty and look at works of art together — a real learning experience.

When the painting was finished in mid-September, we had a celebration. Watty had explained to us that the most difficult thing for him as an artist was to know when to apply the final brush strokes, that is, to make that excruciating decision that the painting was really finished. But, indeed, it was finished, and we not only had a remarkable work of art, but a deep and enduring friendship that grew and lasted until the deaths of both Ida and Watty some years later.

It was particularly nice that we would have the opportunity of showing the Watkins *Family Portrait*, as the Detroit Institute of Arts had asked to borrow our collection to show at the museum that September. It was one of 65 paintings that the museum borrowed, calling the exhibition, "Collection in Progress." It was the first time, but certainly not the last, that this huge family portrait by Franklin Watkins was shown to the public, a final coda to a precious summer experience.

While we were so happily involved with a commission for a contemporary painter, we were still pursuing our interest in the works of artists of the eighteenth and nineteenth century. We were learning more and more about the work of Winslow Homer, Albert Ryder, John Singleton Copley and the famous Peale family.

In all of our collecting experience, Larry has always been the catalyst, the driving force — the engine, as it were — that has driven this amazing train. Although I wouldn't particularly call myself the caboose, I have been the enthusiastic follower and co-collector.

To give an example of Larry's persistent "bird-dogging" technique, he heard through Ted Richardson of a portrait that a descendant of the Peale family might possibly want to sell. In no time, the three of us were on a train to Philadelphia to look at the painting. What was so extraordinary was that the woman offering the painting looked so much like her two ancestors in the painting. Shortly thereafter, James Peale's double portrait entered the Fleischman collection.

In January 1956, a group of our paintings was borrowed by the Kalamazoo Art Center with works of art from the collection of Eleanor and Bill Poplack, a couple whom Larry had encouraged to buy American paintings.

Through the Art Adventurers activities interest had grown so much in American art that Larry spawned another idea. He recruited five other Detroit couples to plan a one-day art show and sale in Detroit, bringing the New York art world to our home city. Our partners were Marianne and Alan Schwartz, Reva and Al Taubman, Toba and Bert Smokler, Eleanor and Bill Poplack, and Edna and Ben Goldstein.

In no time we put together a purse for expenses ($25 per couple), persuaded the Goldsteins to host the event (they owned a handsome suburban home designed by the architect Minoru Yamasaki) and set the date for a day in May 1956. Then, Larry went to work with his art dealer contacts in New York to select a heterogeneous and interesting group of paintings, none costing more than $500, and ship them out to Detroit.

Our little committee banded together to send out invitations to our guest list, buy some wine to serve, purchase the materials for mounting and hanging the works of art, and set up a payment system whereby the purchasers would make their checks out directly to the gallery owners.

The day dawned beautifully and throughout the afternoon several hundred eager would-be collectors walked through the entire house examining the paintings. To the utter delight of the "committee," a large number of the paintings were sold, making it unnecessary to send many back to the gallery owners in New York City.

What was particularly amusing was to see such busy and successful professional men and women of our committee working so hard to hang, present and sell the works of art. Their enthusiasm was infectious.

Everyone was exhilarated — the purchasers with their new treasures, the committee with its great success, and, of course, the dealers, sensing some incipient collectors.

The costs were so low, owing largely to the volunteers' hard work, that all of us were able to take what money was left over and treat ourselves to a celebratory dinner at a nearby restaurant.

There were far-reaching implications for this amusing project, as a good number of the people who made their first important purchase of an original work of art (such as a small Burchfield watercolor, a small Marin print or a Childe Hassam drawing) went on to form collections of American art. Larry's idea had been to demystify the purchase of an original work of art and remove the intimidation some felt in going to a commercial gallery. This suburban art show accomplished his aim completely.

As a matter of fact, the word of this show spread so positively that about a year later the same group repeated the event, this time including the work of local Michigan artists, and upping the top price to $1,000. It, too, was a roaring success.

Another activity in the Detroit art world that commanded Larry's attention was the Detroit Society for Arts and Crafts. It was the oldest art school in Michigan, having been established in 1906, incorporated in 1915, and becoming a full-fledged art school in 1926.

Larry had become the treasurer of the school and, working with Walter B. Ford II and Wendell W. Anderson, Jr., began to effectuate some changes and improvements in the administration of the school. A pension plan and insurance coverage were initiated. In 1958, a new building, designed by Minoru Yamasaki was dedicated.

To celebrate the 50th anniversary of the school, Wayne University Press published a book titled *Art and the City*, written by Joy Hakanson Colby, art editor of the *Detroit News*. In her acknowledgments she stated, "We owe the existence of this book to Lawrence A. Fleischman who encouraged me from the very beginning."

During these years Larry began to be called upon to speak, mostly on the challenge and fun of collecting American art, in such places as Windsor, Ontario, Toledo, Ohio, and for various organizations in the Detroit area, such as the Detroit Chapter of Brandeis University and the Henry Ford Museum Antiques Forum in Dearborn, Michigan. He was correctly dubbed an Ambassador of American art and continues to this day to play that role.

CHAPTER 5

Detroit Institute of Arts

LARRY'S STIMULATING EXPERIENCE IN WORKING ON THE INTERNATIONAL Carpet Design Competition in concert with the Detroit Institute of Arts brought him one of the most significant relationships of his entire life. He became acquainted with Edgar P. "Ted" Richardson, the director of the museum, and they formed a remarkable friendship that grew with the years.

Richardson, a slim, mustachioed man was an impeccable scholar, an expert in American art and a connoisseur of Flemish art. His general knowledge was so profound and deep that one could learn from him on a vast variety of subjects.

He was primarily a shy, reserved and private man; but when one broke through that veil of privacy one found a passionate and committed person with a wry sense of humor. His interests ranged from the ships that traversed the Detroit River, ancient bronzes, American history, to the varying landscapes of the United States, geodes and especially the written word.

Somehow or other he found a kindred spirit in Larry whose background and training were so different from his. From the time they became acquainted he truly became Larry's mentor. Although he was basically a quiet man, his learning and interests were so varried that this unlikely duo was indeed bonded.

His wife Constance was a skilled and gifted landscape painter, a red-headed lady with a wicked and penetrating sense of humor who shared Ted's interests and life with great zest. Between the two of them, many new aspects of life were opened up to us in the most wonderful way, and we treasured the relationship. We continue our warm friendship with Constance to this day.

We began to take an interest in the Detroit Institute of Arts and its programs. When Bill Woolfenden and Ted Richardson asked us to host a dinner for the jury of the Michigan Crafts Show in 1954, we accepted with alacrity. We had already shown our interest in the world of crafts by offering an annual prize for the best piece of pottery in the exhibit.

It wasn't long before Larry was tapped to be on the committee for the Friends of Modern Art gala featuring a concert by Victor Borge. We began to support the museum in a wider way and as our collection drew the attention of the trustees, we were pleased in 1956 when Larry was invited to be a trustee of the Founders Society, the private arm of the Detroit Institute of Arts. The museum is one of the few city owned and managed museums in the United States, managed by an Arts Commission appointed and empowered by the mayor of Detroit.

The Founders Society, however, is the entity which raises all the private moneys which flesh out and expand the activities, purchases and reach of the museum. Larry immediately became an active member of the Founders Society board and was appointed to be head of the Library Committee. In June 1957, through a combination of gifts of money and works of art, he was named a Benefactor of the museum.

Director Richardson had in the late fifties inaugurated and organized what turned out to be a seminal exhibition, "Masterpieces of Flemish Art," which was sponsored by the Detroit Museum and the museum in Bruges, Belgium. New trustee Fleischman played a tiny but important role in one aspect of this exhibit. As the plans unfolded for the show, the budget for the catalogue was presented to the Founders Society trustees who collectively threw up their hands at the sum of $48,000 which the book was projected to cost. The catalogue was about to be emasculated when Larry gave an impassioned plea to the trustees. He reminded them of the scholarly importance of this catalogue documenting a once-in-a-lifetime exhibition — and indeed of any exhibition. He persuaded them to reconsider, and the catalogue, though now out of print, remains a milestone in art history.

In April 1962, the new mayor, Jerome P. Cavanagh, appointed Larry, who was now 37 years old, to the Detroit Arts Commission with the statement that he wished him to serve as its president, an incredible honor for such a young man. With the announcement of this appointment came a problem.

The museum had long been controlled by a generous but tightly knit group of socially prominent citizens from Grosse Pointe, Michigan. This elegant area of the city was an enclave of privilege and had virtually no Jewish homeowners. It was known at that time for being unwelcoming to citizens other than themselves; so, for some of those people, the appointment of a young, Jewish, up-and-coming businessman to be the president of the Arts Commission was looked upon as an affront.

One of the ways in which the Grosse Pointers felt particularly threatened was due to their loyalty to Robert Tannahill, Mrs. Edsel Ford's cousin. He was a very private man who was a great collector and supporter of the museum. This quiet and fragile man was a member of the Arts Commission, and some worried that he would be pushed aside by a dynamic upstart.

There was a flurry of quiet but firm objection to Larry's appointment in some Grosse Pointe circles, one trustee even saying, "If the mayor makes him president of the Arts Commission, we'll crucify Fleischman!" Needless to say, this kind of response made us uncomfortable and caused Larry to question his decision to accept the appointment. However, Mayor Cavanagh, a young, intelligent and adroit politician, persuaded Larry that this would pass, and indeed, several envoys from the trustees, also Grosse Pointers, came to visit us urging Larry to accept.

After much soul-searching he did accept to serve on the commission but insisted that Bob Tannahill be made president. This gesture was very ameliorating, and the seven member commission began to do its work together amiably. Larry and Bob Tannahill became very good friends once it was realized that they had the same aim and goals for the museum.

In the months following, we learned a lot more about Bob Tannahill's magnificent collection and how he had put it together. Tannahill was a character out of a Henry James novel; a bachelor living in his beautiful home with his collections of French Impressionists, German Expressionists, African art, American paintings, silver, porcelains and magnificent drawings from many countries and eras. In his elegant and reserved way he had been a pioneer in collecting.

During his presidency, Tannahill led the quest for a new director of the museum, Ted Richardson having retired in early 1962. In due course Willis W. Woods, director of the Norton Gallery of Palm Beach, Florida, was hired to take his place.

In the meantime, once he came to know Larry well and thus to trust him, Tannahill decided to step down as president, saying that the position sapped too much of his energy and that he looked forward to an advisory role with Larry, as president. His cousin, Mrs. Eleanor Ford, joined in a chorus of approval of Larry. In July 1962, Larry was indeed elected as leader of the museum.

The new president immediately embarked on a series of innovative plans for the museum and began to breathe exciting new life into the institution. He first created a small group of advisors to the Arts Commission, six important long-time supporters of the museum such as Benjamin Long, Edward Rothman and Alvan Macauley, who would meet with the commission without vote but be able to join in with their ideas. Larry had the mayor issue them official advisors' badges. They were made to feel very important which increased their loyalty and commitment to the many new ideas being put forward.

Larry also developed a new tradition of going down to the City Council when the museum budget was being considered, not only with the director and secretary of the commission but with Arts Commissioners and especially Mrs. Ford. This show of strength and solidarity proved to be a powerful weapon in pleading the museum's cause.

Eleanor Ford was a remarkable woman, a small, comely lady with a warm smile and true grace who was also intelligent and very canny. Although at that time one of the richest women in the world, she had an unaffected, simple, easy charm and warmth. She used her power carefully and quietly and was a generous patron to the museum. Her husband, Edsel, had been president of the Arts Commission, so she had a special affinity and loyalty to the museum.

She responded to Larry's rash of ideas with great enthusiasm and said that she could no longer miss a commission meeting — "They're too much fun!" she said. We, at the same time, were totally captivated by her. She has been a role model for us in all the years since we worked so closely together. We learned a great deal from her marvelous example.

One of Larry's first initiatives was to push ahead with a restaurant in the museum, an idea which had been under consideration for some time. Since I had organized the Volunteer Committee of the Founders Society several years before, he asked me if I would organize such a venture. Consequently, with Rux Chapin, Bishie Beatty and Marge Gillis, a food service for the museum was planned.

In the summer of 1962 we set up a temporary little tea room in the Kresge Court to see what the response would be. We engaged a local caterer to serve a few sandwiches, salads, pastries and beverages, set up a group of tables and chairs and went into business. Despite the unfounded concerns on the part of some curators that they would find peanut butter on the works of art, the little restaurant was an instantaneous success. Obviously, the public had been yearning for a quiet place in the museum to sit down and have refreshments. We kept running out of food, so after several months of this makeshift arrangement, we were authorized to make it a permanent restaurant.

One of the amusing sides of that hectic summer was the sight of those lovely Grosse Pointe ladies working side by side with me scrubbing tables, leaving well-staffed homes to do this menial work. Our enthusiasm was boundless.

A professional catering firm signed a contract to bring in a completely efficient team and an expanded menu. We bought more of the attractive wrought iron chairs and tables that made the court so charming. The restaurant was there to stay.

One of the key problems that faced museum visitors was the lack of parking facilities nearby, so the Arts Commission undertook to solve this problem by having a parking garage built adjacent to the museum. In May of 1963 the groundbreaking ceremony was held, and the garage opened for business in February 1965.

In July 1964, an extraordinary event called the Midsummer Night's Dream Ball took place in the museum. What made this party so exceptional was the fact that the ball committee for the first time included African-Americans from the community. On the evening of the ball, again for the first time, the attendees were made up of black and white Detroiters. The museum, with the assistance of some gifted Detroit decorators, was transformed into a Shakespearean bower, and for dancing we had engaged a young, newly emerging talent to bring his orchestra to Detroit — Peter Duchin.

The guests, a handsomely garbed mixture of Grosse Pointe society plus people from Birmingham, Bloomfield Hills, northwest Detroit and, indeed, central Detroit, mingled graciously and ultimately paved the way for greater participation in museum affairs by the whole community. It was a roaring success in every way.

A special area of concern to which Larry was directing his attention was lack of travel funds for curators. He always felt that the more educated and traveled curators were, the more valuable they were to their departments and to the museum in general. Heretofore, funds for travel had been scarce so now this became a higher priority and, in cooperation with the Founders Society, funds were increasingly found for this purpose.

Working closely with the president of the Founders Society, William M. Day, Larry proposed selecting new trustees from a broader spectrum of the city — and indeed, this happened. In October of 1962, a plan spearheaded by Larry was promulgated and revealed to the press for the expansion of the Detroit Institute of Arts. It was the concern of the leaders of both the Arts Commission and the Founders Society that lack of space had become such a problem that the museum was in danger of losing potential private collections. The city administration agreed to look at plans for building two new wings of the museum with great seriousness despite the economic constraints hampering the city.

While these matters were being considered, Larry learned from a casual conversation with Fred Romanoff, an advisor to the mayor, that there existed something called the Accelerated Public Works Act whereby the federal government would give to city projects monies for improving their local facilities. Immediately, Larry asked if the Detroit Institute of Arts, being a city museum, qualified under this act. After swift investigation it was determined that indeed, just like city sewer improvements or street repairs, a city museum was eligible.

The catch was that by the time Larry had by chance learned of this possibility, there were only three more days before this act would expire. With characteristic drive, tenacity and optimism, he devised a plan and immediately called his ardent supporter, Mrs. Edsel Ford. He outlined the possibility for obtaining funds stating that the government would give the museum $1,850,000, but matching funds were required. He had already learned from Mayor Cavanagh that those funds were impossible to get from the local government. However, Mayor Cavanagh said, "Larry, if you can quickly find matching private funds for a South Wing, I promise you that the city will provide the funding for a North Wing."

Larry told Mrs. Ford, "Eleanor, since time is of such an essence, if you could loan us a million dollars immediately, I promise you I'll mount a drive to raise the needed private $1,850,000. Her instantaneous reply was, "Larry, after all you and the others are doing for the museum, I'll give you a million dollars!"

Larry was so stunned by this generous response that, after thanking her profusely, he called the mayor. Explaining what had happened, he told the mayor, "Jerry, call Mrs. Ford immediately to thank her so that I can really believe what I heard!"

And, indeed, it was true, the deadline was met, the additional private funds raised, and the plans for the South Wing of the museum were put into effect immediately.

A touching and revealing incident occurred as the wing neared completion. A deputation including the mayor, Larry and several other art commissioners and politicos met with Mrs. Ford to tell her that they wished to name the new wing for her and her late husband, Edsel. This incredible and modest lady quickly declined saying, "After all, I only provided the money. You're the ones who are doing all the work.!" Larry reported that even the hard-bitten pols were visibly moved by her response.

Excitement ran high at the museum with planning for expansion, new and important acquisitions and the inclusion of more people from various parts of the community. A sense of mission and esprit de corps pervaded the various committees of the institute. Larry worked very well with Willis Woods, the amiable director, who was greatly interested in contemporary art but was able to develop an overview of the entire collection of the museum.

There was one unpleasant episode that slightly marred but did not spoil all the fun. An extremely destructive and jealous man who was not a real part of the "museum family" enjoyed stirring up controversy at some of Detroit's institutions. Chafing because he was not intimately involved at the museum, he went to the *Detroit News* with the story about a magnificent painting by the Dutch seventeenth century artist, Gerard Ter Borch that Larry had heard was on the market and the museum subsequently purchased.

The story that he put forward was that this painting had been languishing on the London art market for many years at a lesser price than what the Detroit Institute of Arts had ultimately paid for it. This question was aired in the newspaper much to our shock, the implication being that perhaps Larry had been involved in this transaction for his personal gain.

We had never been confronted with such a terrible, albeit subtle, accusation and were deeply upset by the whole thing. Of course, when the newspaper did some investigation, it found that the painting had never been on the art market but had been in the Rothschild collection for many years and had just been offered for the first time. So the whole false story fell apart.

In the midst of this brief unpleasantness, Larry was comforted and cheered by the complete support of everyone at the museum including Eleanor Ford who so very uncharacteristically said, "Larry, that's the price you pay for being on top at the museum. When next you see that man, spit in his eye!"

During his tenure as president of the Arts Commission, Larry was occasionally called upon to help the mayor in matters outside of art. The most dramatic instance of this was on the occasion when Martin Luther King was coming to Detroit for a march. Mayor Cavanagh, wanting to defuse what might have turned into a confrontation, set about to welcome Reverend King and asked various of his commission presidents to join him.

While there was some concern at the prospect of a crowd of thousands which could get out of hand, but Larry eagerly went to City Hall to participate in the march and program. Among the vast gathering of black citizens there were only about 30 white people. The event went off beautifully with great spirit and congeniality and was deemed a complete success.

On February 12, 1965, just two days before Larry's 40th birthday, the dedication of the museum's new parking garage took place. In June of that year as the South Wing was steadily moving towards its completion, a festive groundbreaking ceremony took place on the north lawn of the Detroit Institute of Arts. Mayor Cavanagh and Larry were joined by Roger L. Stevens, then the Chairman of the National Council on the Arts, to celebrate the beginning of construction of the North Wing of the museum

By November 1965, the mayor was so encouraged by the enthusiasm and activity at the Detroit Institute of Arts that he created a Community Art Council of 21 outstanding Detroit cultural leaders for the expansion of Detroit's Cultural Center and appointed Larry to serve on the council.

During this period, although mostly involved with museum activities, we were involved in a small way with show business. Larry's friend, the banker Stanford "Bud" Stoddard, sent him a script for a movie that a friend was producing. It was a low budget film called *The Head That Wouldn't Die*, and the costliest item in its budget was the creation of the monster. The script was corny to say the least, but because of Stoddard, Larry decided to invest a tiny amount in the project. A short time later when Larry ran into Stoddard and told him of his participation he asked how much Stoddard had contributed. The conservative banker replied immediately, "Oh, it's too risky — I wouldn't invest!" Amazingly enough, *The Head That Wouldn't Die* became something of a cult movie and made a profit.

In 1961, George C. Scott decided that he wanted to start a repertory company in the Detroit area where he had been raised. He called it "Theater of Michigan" and procured initial backing from the American Broadcasting Company for whom he was doing a weekly series. We became involved in raising funds for this most worthy venture and started to interest our friends in the effort. Scott brought Colleen Dewhurst, Theodore Mann and Jose Quintero into Detroit to help work on the company. Money was raised and several productions mounted. However the time was not ripe for the city to support such an organization, and sad to say, its life was a short one.

However, Larry's ideas for improving and enhancing the working of the museum continued apace. He proposed the idea of taking members of the Arts Commission and Founders Society board to a "working seminar" on museums to be held in London. He organized a program with visits and tours of the National Gallery, Tate Museum, British Museum, Wallace Collection and other institutions, including conferences with their leaders. In this way it was fascinating to learn how different institutions function and cope with their operating problems.

In January 1966, 27 of us arrived in London for a few days of intense educational activity leavened with lots of fun. The participants returned to Detroit with many new insights into the varying ways in which other art institutions work and the additional treat of behind-the-scenes looks at major works of art being interpreted by major scholars. That intense education proved invaluable to them all.

For some years Larry had become increasingly frustrated and unhappy with his livelihood. With a controlling and dominating father at the helm of the Arthur Fleischman Company, there had been little opportunity for Larry to use his creative and leadership qualities in the day-to-day management of the business.

Some years before, in the early days of building our American collection, his father had come to the house and threatened to have a crew pack up the paintings and send them back to the galleries in New York. He stated, "You haven't asked me for money to pay for this collecting yet, but I don't think you should be buying paintings!" Of course Larry refused to acquiesce to this demand, but the fissure between Larry and his father was growing.

Subsequently, to try to bring Larry to heel, his father sent him a letter through the mail cutting his salary in half; now Larry's yearly paycheck from the business would be $6,000. Instead of submitting to his father's attempt to dominate our life and activities, this punishing gesture emancipated Larry from his father's control and gave him the chance to branch out and find other ways of enlarging his income, supporting his family and becoming completely independent. It was New York and the art world that beckoned.

On various occasions Edith Halpert, George Wildenstein, Otto Gerson and other dealers had urged Larry to consider becoming an art dealer, wedding his passion for American art and his skills as a salesman and joining the fray in New York City. By the time 1963 rolled around, we were talking about a move seriously and an opportunity presented itself whereby Larry could obtain a half interest in Kennedy Galleries, an old-time gallery which had been established in 1874. It dealt primarily in prints and also in traditional nineteenth century American pictures.

Our decision was put on the back burner due to two factors. First of all, Larry's father had developed some serious financial problems because of an investment in a high-rise luxury apartment building that he had undertaken to build on his own. He had taken most of the profits from an investment which Larry had initiated and embarked on what proved to be a disastrous project.

The building, called the Jeffersonian, was on the Detroit River. Larry's father perceived it as his monument, but the project had several elements which made it a risky venture. His first mistake was selecting an architect he knew who had never designed such a building. Then, his stubborn inability to listen to Larry's or anyone's ideas or advice made for problems due to his lack of sophistication in these matters. Misjudgments on the part of the FHA which was involved in the project, overruns and several delaying strikes all compounded the problems.

Larry's father made the family increasingly vulnerable by investing more and more of the family assets into what turned out to be a bottomless maw, and he ultimately lost the building and most of the family interests. In the spring of 1964, quite suddenly — and ironically — Larry's mother who had worried endlessly about the outcome of the project, suffered a stroke at the dedication of this ill-fated building. She died several days later. Thus, it became impossible to leave Detroit at that time, and we postponed our move.

Two years later, while we were both working hard on the plans for the dedication of the South Wing of the Detroit Institute of Arts, we made the firm decision for Larry to join Kennedy Galleries, and the announcement was made.

Our life in Detroit ended officially on the exciting note of the opening of the South Wing. I had been appointed as coordinator of the dedication which began with a gala dinner. Eleanor Ford and Bob Tannahill were the co-chairmen of the five days of events which began with a formal dinner and continued with a series of tours, seminars and receptions for all parts of the community. All of these occasions were attended not only by Detroiters but also by distinguished and celebrated people who came from all over the world.

The formal dinner which launched the dedication was a handsome, glittering affair that showed off the new addition to the museum in its full glory, and each patron was given a hand-signed print by Alexander Calder as an important memento of this significant event in the cultural history of Detroit.

After the dust had settled on all of the dedicatory events, a most special and beautiful dinner was given in our honor at the museum, hosted jointly by the Arts Commission and the Founders Society of the Detroit Institute of Arts. Larry was toasted by one and all for the key role he had played in the museum over the years, especially as its leader. We left the evening in a glow of well being and praise as we prepared to end this chapter and begin a new life in New York City.

CHAPTER 6

WITI-TV

LARRY'S CONNECTION WITH MICHIGAN POLITICS BEGAN WHEN HE WAS elected a precinct delegate about 1951. Although he was quickly disillusioned when he observed that the results of the election were announced before the ballots were counted and didn't feel encouraged to continue his so-called political career, he met a fine man who was deeply involved in the Democratic party, Donald M.D. Thurber. Donald was an unusual breed, a Democratic Grosse Pointer, who, although already a successful lawyer with a prestigious Detroit law firm, was a devoted liberal.

Through his acquaintance with Thurber, Larry was introduced to a bright, handsome and charismatic newspaperman, Blair Moody, who had been appointed by Governor G. Mennen "Soapy" Williams to the Senate to fill the unexpired term of the late Senator Arthur Vandenberg. Blair and Larry quickly became fast friends despite the difference in their ages; both had enormous energy, lots of good ideas and the tenacity to follow them through. Through our acquaintance with Blair, we soon found ourselves in the thick of the 1952 Adlai Stevenson campaign for the presidency, raising money from our friends and acquaintances through such devices as hosting a reception featuring Senator Paul Douglas from Illinois.

However, there were soon other interesting irons in the fire; Blair had the dream of publishing a liberal newspaper in Detroit and in August of 1953, organized a small group to try to bring it to reality. The first step was the purchase of a local printing company, Michigan Rotary Press, with the plan of operating it until it was stable and then expanding it into a small newspaper. The idea was basically a sound one since Detroit's three newspapers, the *Detroit News*, the *Detroit Times* and the *Detroit Free Press*, were all conservative Republican papers.

Among the few joining in this venture were Larry, Ann Hart (the wife of the respected Senator from Michigan, Philip A. Hart) and Donald Thurber. Larry, with the others, threw himself into this project with typical verve and enthusiasm and became its treasurer. Larry was further introduced to the vagaries of Democratic party politics through Blair, attending with him the Democratic party dinner in Chicago where he met Roger L. Stevens, a real estate investor and theatrical producer who was a power in the party.

As a sidelight, the acquaintance with Stevens led to our participating as angels in several Broadway productions with which he was involved. The Playwrights Company involved us in Elmer Rice's *The Winner*, which, unhappily, did not live up to its title and closed out of town. Next, we invested in a beautiful play, *In the Summerhouse*, which received good reviews but didn't last. Finally, we bought a share in *Ondine*, an enchanting play starring Audrey Hepburn as a mermaid. She was ravishing and the play a huge success, but she was in love with her leading man, Mel Ferrer, who persuaded her to marry him during the run of the play. It closed before it could make a profit for the investors.

Larry also bought a share in the Squibb Building on the corner of Fifth Avenue and 58th Street through a syndicate which Roger Stevens organized, and he kept this investment until its sale some years later.

That November, shortly after the long-overdue birth of our daughter, Martha, in October, we were invited to the annual Gridiron Dinner in Washington where the press lampoons and satirizes the political world. Although the dinner itself was at that time still a stag occasion, there were many other events for the wives to attend, and we both thoroughly enjoyed the heady atmosphere of the political world.

At about that time, on a plane from Washington to Detroit,

Blair heard a conversation about a television license that was about to be available for new ownership. He quickly told Larry about it and they initiated plans to try to apply. The VHF station was in Whitefish Bay just outside of Milwaukee, Wisconsin, and was most attractive as an investment. So, Blair and Larry went to Washington to consult an attorney specializing in this still-fledgling field of television ownership. They then began to put together a group of investors including Larry's father and Max Osnos, a local businessman and philanthropist. Larry went to the Wabeek Bank in Detroit and obtained a loan for the seed money to begin the venture.

At the same time, Larry was advised that it would be a more successful and important strategy for getting the license if they were to enlist Milwaukee investors, too. When the partners agreed, Larry used some of his contacts in the Detroit Jewish community to arrange a meeting with some key people in the Milwaukee community, headed by Sol Kahn who was then president of the Jewish Welfare Federation.

A luncheon meeting was arranged in Milwaukee and Larry went there with young Blair Moody, Jr., in tow to "make the pitch." It is amusing to note that during the meeting one of the Milwaukeeans excused himself from the room to make a secret phone call to one of his acquaintances in Detroit asking, "Do you know this wild young Fleischman from Detroit? Is he for real?"

He was quickly reassured that Larry Fleischman was indeed a substantial community person and "for real." So the gentlemen around the table, responding to Larry's enthusiasm, immediately joined the investment group which they named Independent Television Company. Among them, in addition to attorney Sol Kahn, were Jack Kahn, president of Holeproof Hosiery and the Fried brothers, local businessmen. Robert K. Straus of New York City joined the group later.

For the next year and a half, the group worked assiduously with the Washington media lawyer Colonel Roberts, invested funds steadily and met frequently to make their case for ownership of the station.

One of the most difficult aspects of this undertaking was

the difficult task of fighting the formidable and powerful Hearst Corporation headed by Richard Berlin, which was itself determined to win this attractive license. The unpleasant and insidious senator from Wisconsin, Joseph P. McCarthy, had unsuccessfully tried to persuade the Federal Communications Commission to grant the license immediately to the Hearst Corporation, but he had been turned down. It was soon characterized in the press as "the hottest licensing fight in the nation."

Tragically, in this venture and Michigan Rotary Press, Blair Moody was not to live to see fulfillment. In 1954, he began to run on his own for the senatorial seat but was unexpectedly opposed in the Democratic primary by a "spoiler," Patrick McNamara. Blair campaigned very hard throughout the entire state of Michigan and suffered a fatal heart attack while on a swing through upper Michigan, dying there at the age of 52.

Although this was a great personal loss to us and especially to Larry, his friend and working partner, the battles to make Michigan Rotary Press profitable and to gain ownership of Channel 6 in Whitefish Bay, Wisconsin continued.

After a long and hard fight, the FCC awarded the license for the station to Independent Television Company in June 1955. What apparently weighed heavily in the balance for Larry's group was the presence of local and substantial Milwaukee ownership. Sol Kahn became chairman of its board and Larry its treasurer. Thus, WITI-TV was born and, having purchased state-of-the-art equipment from the Dumont Corporation, may well have been the first television station in the country to broadcast in full color.

In great triumph, our entire family wended our way to Milwaukee in May 1956, for the celebratory dedication of the station. The children, in particular, were especially thrilled to witness the production of the local children's show, complete with clowns, from inside the studio.

This fascinating investment began to do well immediately. It was a matter of great pride to Larry and the partners. In 1957 the George Storer Corporation offered an enormous amount of money for the station. The partners had made an agreement that if ever an offer were made to buy them out, it could be turned down if the partners could match the price. In this case, the price was so large that it simply could not be met by the partners of Independent Television Company so, with greatly mixed feelings, they sold the station to Storer.

Having made so many friends in the Milwaukee community, we were delighted when Edward Dwight, the director of the Milwaukee Art Center, asked to borrow some of our art collection for an exhibition. On March 3, 1960, it opened at the museum. It pleased us to share our collection with members of a community with which we had business dealings and so many pleasant associations. The exhibit was wonderfully received by Milwaukee and attracted great crowds.

With the death of Blair Moody, the spark plug for a liberal newspaper in Detroit — the drive, to some extent — went out of Michigan Rotary Press. Although it continued to function as a printing plant for some time, the partners, headed by Donald Thurber, had little interest in merely operating a printing plant. In the fall of 1958, Michigan Rotary Press was sold to its vice president and general manager, and although a profit wasn't realized, the partners came out with their investments intact.

Thus it was that Larry's careers as a television station operator and a publisher of a liberal Detroit newspaper both came to end. Nonetheless, this was an exciting, exhilarating and educational chapter while it lasted, with friendships that continued over the years.

CHAPTER 7

Archives of American Art

As COLLECTING AMERICAN ART BECAME AN IMPORTANT FOCUS OF LARRY'S life, learning about American art was a pertinent prerequisite of this interest. As he tried to delve deeper into the lives of American artists who were no longer alive, he became increasingly frustrated.

One of the artists who seemed fascinating was John Quidor, several of whose evocative paintings in his "Sleepy Hollow" series we owned. However, outside of the facts that he had been born early in the nineteenth century in Tappan on the Hudson River and often painted fire engines for a living, little was known about him.

On a rainy Saturday afternoon in early 1954, Larry sat me down and unfolded an idea that he had been turning over in his mind. Since our country was so large and the papers and memorabilia of artists were thus so scattered geographically, what did I think about the creation of an organization that would bring all these items together in one place so that scholars could study them in an organized way? He was not a little irked that since World War II, approximately 170-some books had been written about Pablo Picasso while perhaps only nine or ten books had been written in the entire field of American art. Perhaps, he reasoned, if scholars with their limited financial means could find their source material in one place, they would be more likely to embark on books about American art.

My reaction was immediate and I encouraged him to go quickly to Ted Richardson to see if this outstanding scholar in the field would react as positively as I did. So, without delay, he called Richardson and immediately drove to his home.

Ted's reaction was the same as mine but, being a professional, he added another ingredient to this new idea and the use of a new tool — microfilm. In that way, he said, if one couldn't have the original material of an institution or artist, one could have it on microfilm.

With great excitement, Larry and Ted proceeded to organize this idea, flesh it out and present it to the powers-that-be at the museum so that it could be turned into reality. A place was found for its office within the Detroit Institute of Arts, and it was announced to the public in June 1954. Larry and I donated a check in the amount of $100 to establish a bank account until funds could be raised in an organized way.

Richardson had urged that this institution be called the Fleischman Archives of American Art but Larry declined, citing the example of the Whitney Museum in New York whose name always gave the impression to the public that it was fully funded by the Whitney family. So, they named it the Archives of American Art, and we donated its first holdings, a group of letters from artists.

It was officially and legally chartered on November 17, 1955, and a most imaginative and lively board of trustees was formed. By the time it was completely organized, the board consisted of cartoonist Al Capp; actor-collector Vincent Price; Mrs. Charles F. Willis of the Firestone family; collectors Henry duPont, Howard Lipman and Joseph Hirshhorn; Senator J. William Fulbright; and Detroit lawyer, Frank W. Donovan. The chairman was Ford Motor Company executive Charles Moore, Mrs. Edsel Ford was appointed vice chairman, Larry was treasurer, and Ted Richardson became its director.

Now, the challenge was to raise the money to begin the work of gathering and microfilming material on American art from all over the country. Mrs. Ford supported the Archives from its very inception and gave it its first significant financial boost and soon the group developed a myriad of inventive ideas to introduce this new institution to the public and encourage donations.

The first Archives of American Art newsletter was published in December 1957, and reported many activities and much progress in getting more visibility for this project which already had over 200,000 microfilmed documents in hand. Miriam Lesley and Bartlett Cowdrey, two very able scholar/archivists had begun duplicating the records of the American Philosophical Society in Philadelphia and the Downtown Gallery in New York City, and a strategy was being set up to microfilm and gather material in an efficient and orderly way. The scope of the Archives had been clarified to include American craftsmen and designers as an important part of the American creative community.

Two fundraising receptions had been organized in the homes of Detroit art collectors, one featuring Vincent Price as the guest speaker and the second "starring" Al Capp, both of whom, as trustees, spoke emotionally about the need for the Archives. These events netted almost $10,000!

Vincent Price was a particularly enthusiastic supporter and booster of the Archives, helping as much as he could from the West Coast. Since he and Larry had the same approach to art and both valued the importance of scholarship and connisseurship, they became special friends. Although our paths didn't cross often enough, it was always a treat to see him.

Through the persuasive offices of Eleanor Ford and Charles Moore, the Ford Foundation made its first gift of $250,000 to the Archives, setting the tone for future gifts from other foundations and corporations to come.

In October 1958, Larry was elected president of the Archives and immediately began expanding its initiatives and planning new ones with the aim of establishing regional centers and committees. A dynamic and gifted photographer and public relations man in the art world, Peter Pollock, had been attracted to the project through New York acquaintances, and together with the energetic art collector Eloise Spaeth, concocted a plan to launch a New York chapter.

In connection with the famed "Masterpieces of Flemish Art" exhibition which was on view at the Detroit Institute of Arts, a chartered airplane with some 80 New York art aficionados flew to Detroit, where their full day included luncheon at the museum, a viewing of the show of Flemish paintings and sculpture, a tour of the Archives office and cocktails at the home of Eleanor Ford.

They returned to New York City that evening with an enhanced understanding of the importance of the Archives. The Archives coffers were also enhanced with the donated dollars of the New York travelers.

This "airlift" was such a success in every way that Larry and Peter Pollock sat down together to see how it could be adapted to bring in more dollars and interest for the institution. Thus, the "airlifts" to Europe, Asia and many parts of the globe benefiting the Archives were born (which have, incidentally, continued all through the years to the present and have served as blueprints for other organizations).

In the meantime, the American Institute of Decorators, through several of its constituents who were Archives members, organized a sale and auction of 1,500 works of art and decorative objects for the benefit of the Archives. An enthusiastic committee brought this to fruition in November 1960, netting $60,000.

Through all these activities and the interest engendered throughout the Detroit community, new people were being attracted to the "fun" of raising money for the Archives. One such person was Harold O. Love, a bright, smart and forceful attorney who was active in symphony circles. He and Larry struck up a friendship, and he joined the Archives team with great verve, becoming the chairman of the Detroit chapter.

In a short time, with ideas flowing a mile a minute, Harold planned a gala Lundi Gras dinner to be held at the renowned London Chop House restaurant to attract the social part of the community to the Archives. Since the first dinner in 1961, this has been an annual, lively, delicious and moneymaking evening which continues to this very day. A few months later, Cornelia Otis Skinner came to Detroit to give a benefit performance which netted more dollars and visibility for the Archives.

In September, the first European Archives airlift took off with a full contingent of art lovers from all over the country filling a chartered KLM plane, and headed for Amsterdam, Rome, Paris and London. The concept of the special trip which made it so attractive to otherwise sophisticated travelers was the opportunity of visiting collections not generally open to the public and in many ways getting a behind-the-scenes view of the art world in all of those famous capitals. So, for a special contribution to the Archives over and above the price of the trip, all these special arrangements and introductions were made possible through the contacts of the various committee members.

Through the years of all of these trips amidst lost luggage, found friends, romances kindled, amazing sights seen, art and souvenirs purchased, the Archives has increased its income. We were even trapped temporarily in Barcelona during the Cuban missile crisis with only sketchy knowledge of what was going on in the rest of the world. However, the steady annuity accruing from the trips has helped the continuation of its important work.

During the Christmas holidays of 1962, the Fleischman and Love families, all nine of us, embarked on a special mission to Rome. Larry and I had become interested in the work of the excellent nineteenth century expatriate painter, Elihu Vedder and had learned through a Vedder scholar, Regina Soria, that his papers and even some of his work might still possibly exist in Rome. Therefore, we planned our European holiday with the children to have as its finale some art history detective work in Rome. We were thrilled and delighted to find that Vedder's papers and work had not been destroyed after his death in Rome in 1923. They were still stored in old trunks in an apartment just above the Caffe Greco on Via Condotti in Rome. We arranged the purchase, brought them triumphantly back to Detroit where the Love and Fleischman families gave the archival material to the Archives and divided the works of art between us.

The Archives continued to grow and expand and became an important scholarly force in the field of American art. All of a sudden it became clear that the authors of every book being written in that field were depending heavily on the Archive's holdings. This fact encouraged living artists, collectors, dealers, craftsmen and scholars to deposit their papers and memorabilia with the Archives. The auctions, airlifts, benefits and dinners all continued, and slowly Boston, California, and other geographical areas joined Detroit and New York in broadening the breadth of the Archives.

Harold Love conceived of an unusual avenue for raising funds. He had some business interests and many friends in the automotive world and its corollary of the manufacturing of machinery, so he organized a machinery auction for the Archives which, too, was a great success.

Along the way William F. Woolfenden had been persuaded to leave his position as the head of the Education Department of the Detroit Institute of Arts and take Ted Richardson's place as director of the Archives.

In July 1963, a Rome office was opened to deal with all the material that could be found of American painters who had spent many years in Rome, and the Archives continued to grow and flourish.

When we were about to move to New York in 1966, Larry resigned as president of the Archives of American Art, still retaining an active interest in its growth and future, and continuing as an honorary trustee.

On May 4, 1970, the Archives became a part of the Smithsonian Institution in Washington, taking its place with other distinguished and important institutions — and all of this because Larry was curious to learn more about the life of the painter, John Quidor!

CHAPTER 8

United States Information Agency

AN EXCITING NEW CHAPTER OPENED IN LARRY'S LIFE IN APRIL 1956, WHEN he received a letter from Theodore C. Streibert, Director of the United States Information Agency in Washington. It said in part, "When we learned of your private collection that includes eminent examples from Colonial times to the present, we immediately decided it would be ideal for showing the people of Latin America that artistic traditions and achievements are highly valued in this country, not only by museums, but by private individuals as well.

"With this in mind, I should like to request on behalf of the Agency and the United States Government the loan of your collection for a tour of the foremost cities in Central and South America. If you could arrange to be away from your business for sufficiently long intervals, we should also like to have you travel with the exhibition to give lectures and conduct informal discussions. As a young businessman who has assembled an outstanding and representative collection of American art, we feel your presence would make a great contribution to the program effectiveness of the exhibition...."

This was indeed a great honor and challenge for Larry, and we discussed the many ramifications, not only of taking on the complications of loaning the works of art but also his investment of time away from business and family. His innate sense of patriotism played no small part in the decision, and together we determined that it was too great an opportunity to pass up.

He informed Mr. Streibert that we would loan a significant part of our collection and that, indeed, he would be its "ambassador."

In due time plans were formulated, a timetable was set for the tour, the works of art were chosen and a curator from the U.S.I.A. appointed. The exhibit ultimately comprised 57 paintings and six pieces of sculpture, ranging from the work of John Singleton Copley all the way to Charles E. Burchfield, John Marin and Jack Levine. Eva Thoby-Marcelin, a vivacious, petite and dark-haired officer from the Exhibits Division of the U.S.I.A. was the first curator, and Eleanor Powell was its second.

So it was that with much fanfare, bon voyage parties and general excitement, Larry and I departed in August 1956 for Mexico City, the first stop on the 20-month tour. The pattern of activities was set in the Mexico City venue that would apply all through Larry's travels. There were many interviews, a dinner in our honor hosted by the American ambassador, a festive opening of the exhibition at Bellas Artes museum, visits with artists and students, meetings with various intellectuals, a series of lectures by Larry and a formal presentation of the box of the colored slides which he used in his lectures to the museum or an appropriate educational institution.

Larry had carefully selected the slides he used for illustrating his talks to cover many aspects of American art and not only those artists represented in our collection. This gave the assembled audiences a real panorama of the breadth and variety of American art.

It was amusing and diverting for us to be treated somewhat as celebrities during this visit. One young lady, while soliciting my autograph at the Bellas Artes reception stated feelingly, "I'd rather have your autograph than Marilyn Monroe's!" Even taking this enthusiasm with a large grain of salt, it provided us with a lot of chuckles.

We formed a quick friendship with a young "stringer" from *Time* magazine, Richard Oulahan, who had been assigned to write a story about us and this exhibition. He and his wife toured with us all over, introducing us to distinguished artists like Rufino Tamayo and some of the younger Mexican talent as well. Also, the cultural attaché from the American embassy planned a series of excursions and visits which greatly enhanced our understanding of the cultural life of Mexico.

The exhibition apparently broke all records for attendance, which would be the case in almost every city in which the collection appeared. It was obvious that the Latin Americans were hungry to see and learn about the art that was being created in the United States and they were most responsive and appreciative.

A positive and flattering story appeared in *Time* magazine with only one paragraph which irked Larry's mother for the rest of her life. Seemingly, some romantic editor, given the story sent up from Mexico City and reading about Larry's immigrant parents and early frugal life decided to embellish the article and stated that Larry remembered being so poor that the family subsisted for a while on hard-boiled eggs. Since Mrs. Fleischman always prided herself on her cooking and rarely served hard-boiled eggs, she was not pleased at this attempt at romanticizing their early life. This did not prevent us from teasing her thereafter about hard-boiled eggs.

In October, Larry wended his way to Havana, Cuba, for the second showing of the collection. As the first businessman to represent American culture abroad, he took the program planned for him very seriously and tried to feel the political as well as the cultural pulse of each country. In Cuba, many of the intellectuals were talking about the young revolutionary up in the hills, but the American ambassador pooh-poohed the threat of this renegade, Castro, saying that the Cuban government was strong and stable.

We kept remarking to Larry that soon after his trip to one Latin American country or another, there was a shakeup in the government. He humorously assured one and all that he had nothing to do with the volatility and occasional instability of those countries.

Because our children Rebecca, Arthur and Martha were still very young at that time, tempted as I was to accompany Larry on these trips, I opted to stay home for most of them and be "debriefed" when my roving ambassador returned with his many souvenirs and fascinating stories.

More seriously, however, he was debriefed after each trip by the U.S.I.A. and representatives of the U.S. State Department so that they could get his detached and honest view of what he had observed during his stay.

As he continued this remarkable odyssey through the following months, the Fleischman collection made its way to Quito, Ecuador; Bogota, Colombia; Lima, Peru; La Paz, Bolivia; Santiago, Chile; Caracas, Venezuela; Rio de Janeiro, Brazil; Montevideo, Uruguay; and Buenos Aires, Argentina.

When planning the trip to Argentina it was decided that since I was going to be able to accompany Larry, he would arrange some extra stops to give me a broader picture of South America. We started out in Lima because he wanted to share that beautiful city with me and introduce me to the charming new friends he had made on his previous trip.

From there we proceeded to Guayaquil, Ecuador. When the exhibition had been in Quito, some of the people from the museum in Guayaquil made Larry promise that if ever he returned to Ecuador he would give a talk in Guayaquil. We arrived in that steamy, sultry river city and were welcomed with open arms and among many things were shown some of the unique Colonial art of their culture, much of which, unhappily, had suffered as a result of the oppressive humidity.

The new museum was under construction and consequently nothing was on view. However, the director with whom we were visiting asked if we would like to see their collection of Pre-Colombian treasures. When we responded with enthusiasm, he asked his assistant to bring in the objects. She appeared with a tremendous pile of old cigar boxes filled with some of the most beautiful and extraordinary gold and emerald-encrusted jewelry we had ever seen!

After examining all these treasures, aided by the explanations of the director, he reached over to a tattered guest book, blew off the dust and proffered it to us to sign. We were quite amused to see that the last signature before ours was from three years before and was that of Arnold Toynbee.

Soon we were off and flying over the majestic and awesome Andes mountains to Buenos Aires, where the exhibition was opening at the Bellas Artes Museum. All of the accompanying events proceeded flawlessly, and we were fascinated by this Parisian style city with its many citizens of Italian and English background.

During the reception at the museum, while we were standing in the receiving line, Larry felt a tug on his sleeve. Looking down, he spied a pretty young girl who asked, "Are you the Lawrence Fleischman who was in France in the army during the war?"

When Larry said that indeed he had been stationed in France, she, with great emotion, introduced herself as a member of the Jewish-French family that he had befriended when they were nearly starving in a nearby town. Now, by a strange twist of fate, they had found their way to live in Argentina, and seeing Larry's name in the paper, she had come to the museum, hoping he was that soldier from about 13 years before.

She was so excited and insisted we come to their house for dinner some time during our stay. So it was that a few nights later, bearing a chrysanthemum plant for our hostess, we trudged up a winding staircase to their modest apartment. There we met the still-grieving widow and the lively younger daughter and sat down to one of the most poignant dinners we have ever had. It was obvious from the small, stringy chicken and the equally small portion of vegetables served that we were in a home where every penny counted. If ever we had no appetite, this indeed was the occasion.

The mother wept as she tried to express her gratitude to Larry for the role he played in befriending them. It was sobering to us to learn that they were experiencing anti-Semitism in many aspects of their daily life, not the least of which was the difficulty that these bright girls were having in securing higher education.

They explained to us that being Jewish cut them off from the outstanding schools, which would certainly have an adverse effect upon their professional futures. Their stories gave us special insight into the problems of the Jews in South America which later became very well known. Their courage and spirit were amazing, and we were hopeful that things would get better there.

When we returned to Detroit, Larry paid a visit to their well-to-do relatives urging them to take some action to help this beleaguered family. Sadly, it was to no avail — they rationalized that from time to time they sent them packages and they would do no more. We gathered a large group of books that they sorely needed and sent them down to Argentina, but we never heard from the family again and could only wonder from time to time about what had happened to that courageous trio, hoping that they fared well and were able to build a good life.

Larry had a particularly chilling experience when in Venezuela. He had struck up an acquaintance with an Associated Press journalist who invited him to a party inaugurating a newly published book. The book turned out to be written by none other than Juan Peron, the deposed dictator from Argentina. He and his court had taken asylum in Venezuela, from where he was trying to establish a base to return to power.

The experience of meeting him and watching his impact on the group of supporters, several hundred strong, was slightly frightening. Larry said, meeting the dictator, that he had never seen such cold and dead looking eyes as those of Peron, and he was relieved to leave that particular occasion.

The Fleischman exhibition was deemed such an enormous success in all of the cities it visited and Larry's role so key, that in April 1957 he was appointed to the Advisory Committee of the United States Information Agency, a seven-member panel of which he was the youngest. The purpose of this committee was to oversee the work of the agency and play an advisory role in planning the thrust of its exhibitions and work abroad. Larry found this work stimulating and challenging and later, as we shall see, played a role in the debate on censorship of exhibits which emerged at about that time.

The U.S.I.A. was so enthusiastic about the impact of the Latin American tour that they prevailed upon us to extend our loan and send the collection to four international venues. In December 1957 Larry flew to Israel to open the exhibition there, and in the following months, the collection went on to Athens, Istanbul and Reykjavik.

There were many adventures connected with these visits.

In Israel, Larry had a chance to become acquainted with some of his aunts and other relatives who had settled there when his father had emigrated instead to America.

I accompanied him to Greece where the impact of that ancient civilization further enhanced our deep interest in antiquity, an interest which was to emerge full force some 20 years later and change our lives yet again.

In Istanbul, one of his more bizarre adventures was celebrating Halloween by going on a scavenger hunt, sponsored by the U.S. Embassy cultural office. Riding through the darkened and sinister streets of that city, Larry was wedged into a car with his team consisting of Arabs from various countries. All proceeded amicably, and their team won the hunt; however, Larry reported having some anxious moments during the evening.

His anxiety stemmed from the incident when he was lecturing the previous day on the subject of American art. When questions were called, a young Arab stood up and belligerently asked Larry's stance on Israel. Larry quietly asserted his belief in Israel's legitimacy and immediately changed the subject asking for any questions relating to American art; and the subject of Israel was dropped.

He was most fascinated with Iceland and enjoyed that completely literate people and their different life style. It was there that he learned to eat and enjoy fish. He had never liked fish before but, being the guest of honor at various banquets, he was obliged to eat what was placed before him and found to his pleasure that the fish there (netted rather than hooked) was delicious and beautifully cooked.

In March 1958, he received a letter from the new director of the United States Information Agency, George V. Allen, who said, in part, "It has been pointed out repeatedly that one of the most important contributing factors to the success of the exhibition was your personal attendance. Our officers particularly mentioned the easy, friendly way you dealt with all classes and types of people. You and your collection served together as a demonstration that our private businessmen, so commonly believed to be exclusively materialistic, are genuinely interested in the arts."

This letter reinforced our belief that despite the sacrifices of Larry's time and energy in making all these trips, the end result made it worthwhile.

One of the amusing fallouts of his visits to foreign lands was that all of a sudden there began an enormous interest on the part of foreign visitors to make a stop in Detroit. Finally, the State Department and the U.S.I.A., which was issuing travel grants to intellectuals from Latin America and Europe, awakened to the fact that these people were friends Larry had made during his travels. They, on their part, were now curious to visit him and learn what Detroit was all about.

Consequently, we began to have a steady flow of visitors from Mexico, Uruguay, Venezuela, Greece and other far-flung locales, and we set about to show them the merits of the dynamic Motor City. Larry even arranged an exhibition at the Detroit Institute of Arts of the beautiful work of Truman Bailey, a silversmith and sculptor, who had an atelier in Lima, Peru, where, under a Rockefeller grant, he was training the local craftsmen to create works of art from their silver and indigenous stones and gems. He had made so many handsome pieces that Larry felt they should be shown outside of Peru, and sure enough, the small exhibit in Detroit was very warmly received.

The loan of our collection and Larry's participation in the tour received a lot of press in the city and even the rest of the country. On April 30, 1958, the Common Council of the City of Detroit passed a resolution citing "Lawrence A. Fleischman for your outstanding contribution to Detroit's cultural life."

The next year the U.S.I.A. was deep in plans for the "American Way of Life" fair in Moscow's Sokolniki Park. The concept was to show many aspects of American life and it included the setting up of a small house furnished by Sears Roebuck, films showing workers at the Ford automobile plant in Dearborn, Michigan, and a variety of other exhibits reflecting our economy and business and cultural life. One part of the fair was an exhibition of American art, called the "American National Exhibition — 1771-1959," and Larry was very much involved in this project as a committee member.

He was especially fascinated to observe, in working with his like numbers on the Russian side, that often when decisions had been jointly made, the Russian committee members would return the following day having checked with Moscow, and they would completely overturn their previous joint decisions.

A major stumbling block occurred when the Soviet government decided that a catalogue of the exhibition printed by the U.S. government was tantamount to propaganda and would not approve of it. Larry, as president of the Archives of American Art, was called to Washington by President Eisenhower who asked if the Archives, as an outside private organization, would take on the responsibility of printing the catalogue. Also, funding was needed, and Larry agreed to assist in raising money for the catalogue.

There existed at this time an unpleasant miasma of censorship around some of the exhibitions that were being exported by the U.S.I.A. There were certain members of Congress and several conservative and disgruntled Washington artists who took exception to the liberal views of some of the artists represented and sought to exclude them from any overseas, government-sponsored exhibitions.

With this general atmosphere in mind, Larry extracted a promise from President Eisenhower that the Moscow art show would not be subject to this kind of censorship. The jury, which included Franklin Watkins and Lloyd Goodrich, among others, decided that only when the shipment of the works of art was on its way across the ocean would the names of the artists be revealed. When the announcement of artists in the exhibition came, a small but unpleasant and noisy storm of protest erupted in Washington. It was interesting to Larry that several of the academics on the committee ran for cover but people like Watkins and Goodrich stood fast with Larry to quash the protest.

One of the most effective weapons was when Senator Philip A. Hart of Michigan left the senate floor to answer Larry's phone call to discuss the problem. Hart then returned to the floor and gave a most passionate and moving response to those who approved censorship. One of his most telling comments was mentioning how Boris Pasternak was being censored in the

Soviet Union, and he asked the Congress if they wished to approve this same kind of intellectual repression in their own country. His arguments and speech were most effective and telling. The result was that from that time on, the back of the censorship threat was effectively broken.

There proved to be a need for carpeting the art exhibition area, and Larry enlisted his father to get the donation of floor covering. In return, he asked if he could accompany his son to the Soviet Union from which he had escaped so many years before. So it was that in June of 1959 Larry, his father and the art critic Frank Getlein, as well as several Detroit businessmen, made their way to the Soviet Union.

Despite our warnings, Larry's dad persisted in being outspoken in comparing the Soviet Union (unfavorably) to the United States which caused Larry considerable concern. Larry himself was chastised for distributing the catalogues to art schools. He was told that the catalogue could only be shown in the exhibit and that if he continued to distribute them outside of the exhibition area, it could prove unpleasant for him. The exhibit was packed despite the fact that tickets had been carefully and selectively parceled out.

During the protest back in the United States regarding some of the artists represented, the satirical painting by Jack Levine, *Welcome Home*, depicting an unsavory American general, had been singled out to be removed.

In Moscow several rather militant party-liners approached Larry referring sneeringly to that picture. Larry reassured them that indeed the painting was in the exhibition and took them over to see it. When he queried, in return, "Where are your paintings of criticism?" one of them responded quickly, "We have no bad generals!"

Larry was also a witness nearby in the kitchen of the little American house that had been set up at the fair when Vice President Nixon and Premier Khrushchev had their famous disagreement and exchange. It was interesting to Larry to see how adroitly Nixon avoided the area of the controversial paintings and saw to it that he was not photographed at the art exhibit site.

All of his contacts with the Soviets only reinforced his concerns about the Soviet Union and gave him added insights into what life was really like there. He returned home saying he felt like kissing the ground when he arrived because he was so glad to be an American citizen.

This chapter in his life gave Larry incredible experience in dealing with both our government and that of the Soviet Union, immense respect for our career diplomats and a new perspective on his belief in the value of cultural exchanges between countries.

CHAPTER 9

S. S. Atlantic *Cruise*

SEEING THE SUCCESS OF THE ARCHIVES OF AMERICAN ART AIRLIFT TO Europe in 1961, Larry began to nurture another idea to raise money for cultural projects in Detroit.

Wintertime cruises had become more and more popular, and Larry's notion was that there undoubtedly was a market for people who wanted more than the conventional cruise. How would it be, he thought, if in addition to the conventional activities ordinarily arranged on a cruise, there was be a program encompassing art, poetry, drama and even a film festival on board?

Such a program had never been attempted, but he felt it was worth a try. He enlisted the interest of Harold Love, his attorney friend and a local businessman, Leonard Kasle. They incorporated a non-profit entity called the American Cultural Association, Inc., with the idea that any profits from the venture would be divided among several worthy cultural institutions.

They began to put together a program roster with distinguished personalities in the arts and were excited to announce that Cornelia Otis Skinner, the famous actress, writer, and monologist; Lloyd Goodrich, Director of the Whitney Museum in New York and author of books and articles on such figures as Winslow Homer, Thomas Eakins, Albert Ryder; and John Ciardi, the noted poet and poetry editor of *Saturday Review of Literature*, were going to be the "stars" of the cruise.

Larry solicited a loan from his friend and banker, Stanford C. "Bud" Stoddard, and they chartered the S.S. *Atlantic* of the American Export Lines for $260,000 for a 13-day cruise to the West Indies in February of 1962. The project was announced to the press in November 1961, an attractive pamphlet was created enclosing a note from "hostess" of the cruise, Cornelia Otis Skinner, and now all they had to do was to await requests for reservations. Although the ship ordinarily accommodated 900 persons, the trio decided that they would be satisfied if they boarded 550 passengers for this special cruise.

Unhappily, the winter began to unfold as unusually mild and consequently reservations, rather than gushing in, trickled in. This situation called for a new strategy, so it was decided to make visits to key travel agents in various cities to "sell" this unique trip. For a few weeks, the men teamed up and made these calls in the important cities. Soon their efforts bore excellent results.

On February 16, 1962, 550 passengers, including Larry's mother, Bud Stoddard and his wife and Liz Fremd, a reporter sent by *Time* magazine, boarded the S. S. *Atlantic* with great anticipation. The ports of call were San Juan, the port of St. Thomas, Curacao, Kingston and Port-au-Prince — and so the adventure began!

The seas were calm, the weather balmy, and as the cruise proceeded, the program began to unfold. There were certain passengers on board who had simply booked the cruise as a normal vacation, but the rest of the group was fascinated and riveted by the breadth of the program. Larry had even invited Rudolf G. Wunderlich of the Kennedy Galleries in New York to gather a group of works of art to comprise a "floating" exhibit on board and these were duly hung in one of the public salons.

The three partners had obtained some classic films including those of Laurel and Hardy and Charlie Chaplin, plus other famous old movies to create an ongoing film festival. Of course, the cultural "stars" of the voyage performed marvelously throughout the trip. John Ciardi gave a series of poetry readings as well as a seminar based on his book, *How Does A Poem Mean*, which gave the listeners added understanding of the world of poetry. John was a large, ruggedly good-looking man who surprised people because he seemed so unlike the common stereotype of a poet.

Lloyd Goodrich, a spare, mustachioed man who looked the epitome of a Yankee type, delivered a series of illustrated lectures on various aspects of American art and some of this country's famous artists, and Cornelia Otis Skinner performed a series of wonderful readings, both witty and dramatic, adding still more luster to the program.

What was amusing to watch was the bewilderment of those passengers who had joined the cruise for the conventional reasons as they saw this very special program unfolding. We were pleased to gather quite a few converts from this group, adding them to the already exhilarated people who had chosen the cruise for its special program.

As we journeyed from port to port, we attracted much attention from the local press. There were many interviews and appearances on talk shows to explain the reason for planning such a different kind of cruise.

The ship was commanded by an able captain, but one who apparently fancied himself irresistible to the opposite sex. He set out to conquer Cornelia with the offer of tours of the engine room and other remote areas of the vessel. Cornelia, a tall, stately and elegant brunette, handled him with great skill and aplomb, but all of us found his relentless campaign very funny. As a matter of fact, several months later, we had a reunion in New York and learned that the captain had suddenly died on the following voyage. Cornelia responded in her slightly bawdy and wicked way without missing a beat, "In action, I suppose!"

The cruise was filled with lively adventures, the funniest of which took place in Port-au-Prince, Haiti. We had learned that the famous dancer, Katherine Dunham, had purchased an old Bonaparte estate to turn into a resort. She had invited our group, at an added tariff, to spend an evening there with dinner and a dance performance as entertainment. So, a goodly group of us arrived at the lushly tropical estate and sat down to dinner just as the kitchen employees went out on strike. What followed was like a slapstick comedy with other inexperienced staff filling in for the strikers while Ms. Dunham remained in the kitchen to try to complete the cooking.

Some of us were served the dessert first while others were given the first course and then nothing else. To say that the service was sporadic is a masterpiece of understatement. Throughout all this chaos the Haitian dance band played madly, and local citizens invited some of the group to dance; many could be found whirling and twirling on the dance floor to music which never stopped. That evening left an indelible impression upon us which never fails to produce a reminiscent chuckle.

As the cruise drew to a close, the passengers gave the effort most enthusiastic high marks. Incidentally, this kind of "theme" cruise became a forerunner for many popular cruises in the future. We returned to Detroit with the American Cultural Association showing a modest profit, which was divided as planned among several non-profit cultural institutions in the city. All in all, a marvelous adventure and a wonderful time.

CHAPTER 10

The White House

ON OCTOBER 17, 1961, LARRY RECEIVED A CONFIDENTIAL LETTER FROM a James W. Fosburgh inviting him on behalf of Mrs. John F. Kennedy, the new First Lady, to join a small White House Paintings Committee with the goal of procuring paintings suitable and appropriate for this important house built in the year 1791. A bill had been passed by the Congress making the White House a national monument, and Mrs. Kennedy was setting out to give the White House the elegance and splendor that she felt it deserved.

James Fosburgh, a charming man and a serious and excellent painter, was married to Minnie Astor Fosburgh, one of the famous Cushing sisters, and between them they had numerous contacts throughout the social and cultural worlds of New York and the rest of the country. Thus, he seemed a logical choice to help Mrs. Kennedy put the committee together.

Those early days of the Kennedy administration were heady and exciting with new and fresh emphasis on the cultural aspects of our nation. Larry was honored and pleased to be asked to play a role in this project and indicated to Mr. Fosburgh his willingness to join the committee.

In November, he received a gracious note from Mrs. Kennedy inviting him to tea on December 5th when the new committee would be gathering for the first time. In an attempt to have geographical representation on this 11-person committee, Mrs. Kennedy had also chosen Stanley Marcus, Mrs.

William Paley, Joseph Pulitzer, Nathaniel Saltonstall, Mrs. Joseph Alsop, Whitney Warren and Mrs. Morton Zurcher. Henry Francis duPont, who was playing a special role vis-a-vis the furniture and decorative arts donations to the White House, also attended the meeting.

Larry flew to Washington for the December tea where the guidelines were set forth for the gifts and the tax deductibility was reviewed. Jacqueline Kennedy proved to be a gracious hostess whose leadership in this plan would be key to its ultimate success. It was discussed and decided that the committee would operate quietly for the time being, spreading the word in their various communities to interest collectors and other prospective donors in contributing works of art to the White House.

To the surprise of Larry and the rest of the committee, just weeks later it was announced that there would be a tour of the White House on CBS with Mrs. Kennedy showing the new acquisitions. There was some consternation among committee members, but obviously some powers-that-be had decided this would be a great public relations ploy, even though it seemed premature.

Although most of the items shown on the television program had not as yet been acquired, the program was successful in attracting a great deal of attention to the needs of the White House. Despite this change in strategy, the committee forged ahead, and soon many important paintings, prints and drawings began to be donated to the White House.

Larry and I donated two oil paintings on tin, one done in 1835 and the other about 15 years later, showing views of the capitol which carried the signature of Jennens and Bottridge, possibly an architectural firm of the time. They were enthusiastically received by Mrs. Kennedy as most appropriate and interesting for the White House to own.

The excitement and challenge of beautifying the White House continued with another meeting with the First Lady in November 1962, and the contributions continued to flow into Washington. When the new White House guide was published, Mrs. Kennedy sent Larry a handsomely bound and personally inscribed copy which is a treasured part of our library.

Unhappily, with the assassination of the president in 1963, there was a lengthy hiatus in this program, but in March 1964 Larry received a letter from Mrs. Lyndon Johnson stating that President Johnson had issued an Executive Order establishing on a permanent basis the office of the Curator of the White House and the Committee on the Preservation of the White House.

She invited Larry to come to tea on May 7th to discuss the future work of the committee, and when he met with her for the first time, he was completely captivated by her warmth, incisive intelligence and commitment to further the work of Jacqueline Kennedy. In speaking to Larry she admitted to her lack of knowledge of American art, referring innocently to the artist "Homer Winslow," but Larry found her honesty and directness endearing and returned home a complete fan. Several subsequent meetings with Lady Bird Johnson regarding paintings for the White House only served to reinforce Larry's admiration for this amazing woman.

Over the following years we visited the White House on various special occasions in succeeding administrations, but two events in the Johnson administration were most memorable for Larry. The first of these was a White House Festival of the Arts in June 1965 which started at 10 a.m. and continued for the entire day and evening with Mrs. Johnson as its hostess. It opened in the morning with a salute to prose and poetry including readings by Saul Bellow, Catherine Drinker Bowen, John Hersey and Phyllis McGinley. This was followed by Marion Anderson narrating the musical section with performances of the works of American composers such as Ned Rorem, Robert Whitney, Leonard Bernstein and George Gershwin.

Drama followed, introduced by Helen Hayes with excerpts from *The Glass Menagerie*, *The Subject Was Roses*, *Death of a Salesman* and *Hard Travelin'*. The motion pictures were then represented by scenes from *North by Northwest*, *On the Waterfront*, *Shane*, *The Best Years of Our Lives* and *High Noon* with Charlton Heston as narrator.

Dance was chaired by Gene Kelly with the Robert Joffrey

Ballet giving a performance. A jazz section with Duke Ellington as its star followed.

In the evening there was an exhibit of paintings, sculpture and photography featuring works by some of the most distinguished contemporary American artists. Many of these artists and other creative people were in attendance throughout the day, and the entire program left no doubt as to the variety, richness and importance of all of the American arts.

Larry was most struck by Mrs. Johnson's participation: she was in attendance during the entire festival, slipping away briefly just a few times to change her outfit. The symbolism of her imprimatur on the proceedings was not lost on anyone; even President Johnson stopped by to greet all the attendees.

The only fly in the ointment was the sight of the critic Dwight MacDonald passing through the group of distinguished guests attempting to get signatures for a petition against the Vietnam War. Apparently everyone, regardless of their views, felt that this was not the appropriate or even proper occasion on which to voice his dissent and he was firmly persuaded to desist. Regardless, the event had its impact and showed that the administration truly respected and encouraged the arts in the United States.

This festival was followed by Larry's last connection with the White House and the arts when he was invited to attend the signing of the Arts and Humanities Bill on September 29th at the White House. President Johnson directed these important ceremonies. He signed the bill creating the endowments for the Arts and Humanities, and with a flourish gave the first pen to "my most ardent lobbyist," Lady Bird Johnson.

The pen that the president gave to Larry is an object he treasures as a symbol of his activities in connection with arts and the White House, an exciting chapter in his life.

CHAPTER 11

Tombstone, Arizona

ONE OF THE KEY FIGURES IN OUR COLLECTION OF AMERICAN ART WAS John Marin, whose work resonated for us in so many ways. He was completely American and unique in his approach to nature and the city and was a source of stimulation and satisfaction to us. During that time we had gathered what was said to be the largest collection of his work outside of the Phillips Collection in Washington, acquiring oils and watercolors from all phases of his productive life.

Larry had become so involved in the work of Marin that it was no surprise that he was invited by the University of Arizona to speak about the artist in conjunction with an exhibit the university was mounting. Therefore, in March of 1963, Larry went out to a part of the country with which he was only familiar through his addiction to Western movies. After his lecture, the president of the university, Richard A. Havill, asked him if there was anything in that part of Arizona that he'd like to see. Larry quickly responded that he was fascinated by what he heard about Tombstone, Arizona, and would enjoy seeing if it really existed.

Havill arranged to take Larry out to Tombstone, which is just 90 miles south of Tucson and 16 miles from the Mexican border. Soon Larry was caught up in the romance and magic of that dusty old town which had figured so importantly in the lore of the old West. He had known of it as "The Town Too

Tough To Die" where the famous shoot-out at the O.K. Corral had taken place between Wyatt Earp and his brothers, Doc Holliday, the Clantons and MacLaurys.

Seeing it for the first time only heightened his interest. His curiosity was piqued to find out why this bustling and prosperous capital of Arizona in the end of the nineteenth century with its 20,000 citizens, had become a tiny, rather forsaken town of some 1,200 people.

He returned home to Detroit with the fascinating idea of trying to restore Tombstone to some of its earlier glory, making it more of a tourist attraction and, indeed, the "Williamsburg of the Old West!" To that end, he gathered his friends, Harold Love and Wallace Clayton and an acquaintance from Utica, New York, William Murray, to try to persuade them to take on this venture with him. And in this way, Historic Tombstone Adventures was born in January 1964.

Larry's friend, lawyer Harold Love; Wallace Clayton, an executive with J. Walter Thompson advertising agency; and William Murray, a shrewd businessman as well as president of the Munson-Williams-Proctor Museum in Utica, brought many skills and strength to this idea. In no time exciting plans were being made.

The city fathers of Tombstone, the Tombstone Chamber of Commerce and the Tombstone Restoration Commission, welcomed the sincerity and eagerness of these "Easterners" and were most cooperative from the very beginning. In short order Historic Tombstone Adventures had bought 23 acres of Tombstone. The purchase encompassed Schieffelin Hall, the largest adobe building in the world, which had been constructed in 1881. This building had housed touring companies of all kinds, civic meetings, recitals and dances in Tombstone's heyday.

The purchase also included the old Crystal Palace Saloon, the main gathering place of those days, and soon it was being restored with its 45-foot mahogany bar and the reproduction from fragments of the gold and white-eagled pattern of the original wallpaper. The saloon interior soon returned to its colorful handsomeness and the false front of the building reaching to the second floor was entirely restored to its 1880 state. The second floor was where Marshall Virgil Earp, Sheriff John Behan and others had had their offices.

Larry and his friends engaged a young historian from the staff of the University of Arizona to delve deeply into the history of this wonderfully eccentric town, and he began to turn up new facts in its amazing story.

This quartet of "new Westerners" proceeded to restore the infamous O.K. Corral, and Larry persuaded his friend Vincent Price to narrate the audio-visual presentation which had been newly created. At the rear entrance of the O.K. Corral they discovered the old photo gallery and studio of Camillas S. Fly called "the Matthew Brady of the West." They arranged a permanent exhibit of as many of his old photographs as could be found, in addition to his mural-size prints. These gave a vivid picture of the town in the era of the 1800s.

In those days, Tombstone was an amazingly sophisticated town with five newspapers, many and varied civic activities, a French club, theater performances and even elegant prostitutes brought over from France! Cornelia Otis Skinner told us that her father, Otis Skinner, had performed there, and there were clippings and posters to show that Eddie Foy and The Seven Little Foys and many other famous vaudevillians had included Tombstone on their circuit.

Tombstone had been founded by Frank Schieffelin when, as a young scout for the army, he had hidden in the Arizona hills when being chased by Indians. Upon examining several of the rocks in his hiding place he saw what he believed to be strains of silver ore. This so excited him that he resigned his job saying that he was going to look for silver. His friends told him that the only thing he would find in those Arizona hills would be his tombstone!

He indeed found silver in abundance and named the tiny town he founded — Tombstone. The colorful characters who inhabited the town and gathered on Toughnut Street, its main thoroughfare, were an amazing mix of people, outcasts from other cities, adventurers, miners, desperadoes and folks merely wanting to establish a stable and comfortable community. The Earps, Doc Holliday, Big Nose Kate, Cochise, the Ringo Kid and the lawless gangs who were rustlers and marauders were joined by solid businessmen, and their families of churchgoers. There was even a substantial Jewish community.

The *Tombstone Epitaph*, the Arizona newspaper which has been published for many years, became part of Historic Tombstone Adventures and was revitalized by Wallace Clayton who is its publisher today.

Another tourist attraction that brings interested horticulturists to Tombstone is the largest rosebush in the world which spreads over 5,000 square feet. A slip of this bush was brought to Tombstone by an English mining engineer and his new bride to remind them of the English roses of their homeland. They planted it in what was once a stable, and nature took over. The rosebush is now cared for by the University of Arizona.

The owners of the charming Birdcage Theater were spurred on by all the restoration excitement engendered by Larry and his colleagues and were moved to restore that building, which added to the new luster of the town.

Historic Tombstone Adventures purchased three acres of land near the famous Boot Hill Cemetery overlooking the handsome Dragoon mountains. An architect from Tucson was engaged who designed and built the HTA Motel in the hopes of accommodating the new influx of tourists. The four partners even bought a ranch to show their dedication to the community and as an investment in the area.

With all this activity, Larry was almost becoming a cowboy and took a lot of ribbing. On several of his trips west he began to take early morning horseback rides and became so enthusiastic that, for $200, he purchased a horse named Drake. When asked by the habitues of the Crystal Palace Saloon how old Drake was, Larry hastily returned to the rancher from whom he had bought the horse to ask about Drake's age. Without even removing the long weed that was in his mouth, the tall, rangy rancher replied, "Well, Mr. Fleischman, if horses could collect Social Security, Drake would be the first in line!" Undaunted by this fact, Larry developed a great affection for his sedate steed, especially after having had several experiences on other more lively mounts.

Helldorado is a three-day Tombstone event every October which brings Western buffs from all over to reenact the shoot-out at the O.K. Corral and, in general, relive the old days of Tombstone. The first year that Larry joined the official parade on a unfamiliar horse, he was stationed just behind the high school band. When the cymbals were struck, the horse began to rear. The reviewing stand consisted of the commanding officer of Fort Huachuca, the mayor and other local dignitaries. When they saw Larry hanging on for dear life to the neck of the horse, they howled with laughter thinking that this was a comedy act brought in to enliven the parade.

The next year, the HTA Motel was being officially opened during the Helldorado festivities. In the parade preceding the dedication of the motel, Larry was riding tall in the saddle on old Drake. All went well until Larry looked at his watch and realized that they were running late. Signaling his partner, Harold Love, they turned off Toughnut Street to head for the hotel and found that the parade was mistakenly following them. With great hilarity, all was straightened out and the motel opened with appropriate fanfare.

Our interest in Arizona was sharpened by these projects and the lively exploits of Historic Tombstone Adventures. When we were asked to loan part of our collection for an exhibition at the University of Arizona, we quickly accepted. Under the guidance of Curator William L. Steadman, 106 works of art made their way to Tucson, and the exhibit opened to great acclaim in February 1964. In the first year after all of the newly restored elements of Tombstone reopened, business increased over 20 percent. The community continues to prosper and attract more and more attention each year.

Larry's interest and enthusiasm were unabated, but when in 1966 he made the dramatic move from Detroit to become an art dealer in New York, he realized that all of his attention would have to be devoted to his new career. He divested himself of most of his interests in Historic Tombstone Adventures except for a small percentage in the *Tombstone Epitaph*, which we still read today. Larry always speaks nostalgically and affectionately about his "Tombstone adventure."

CHAPTER 12

Kennedy Galleries

ON JULY 8, 1966, AFTER A FLURRY OF FAREWELL PARTIES IN DETROIT, articles in the Detroit press and the *New York Times*, Larry and I with our children, Rebecca, Arthur and Martha (and dachshund Brandy), made the move to New York City and established ourselves in a duplex at the United Nations Plaza.

We had divested ourselves of the most important part of our collection of American paintings and sculpture for two reasons. Firstly, Larry reasoned, correctly, that if we continued to be collectors in the American fields ourselves, he, as a collector would be tempted to keep the most outstanding examples for our private collection. This would be a conflict of interest in his new role as an art dealer and would certainly not serve his clients in the fairest and most honorable way.

Secondly, the large group of significant works of art served as part of the assets that figured in the partnership agreement. Our outstanding works became a key part of the inventory of Kennedy Galleries enhancing and broadening its scope which had largely been prints, Western paintings and sculpture and some nineteenth century landscapes. The infusion of our great portraits, genre scenes and twentieth century art began to give an entirely new look to the gallery.

Kennedy Galleries had been founded as a small print gallery by Herrmann Wunderlich in 1874. A short time later the ownership was taken over by Edward G. Kennedy after whom it was named. Kennedy was a close friend of James Abbott

McNeill Whistler, and therefore, the gallery was the first to exhibit his etchings and paintings in the United States. Around the time of World War I, the business reverted back to the Wunderlich family until Larry bought a half interest in 1966.

Larry, with his experience as a collector, his keen interest in scholarship through the Archives of American Art, his tenure as a museum president and his abilities as a salesman brought many special skills to his new career.

At this time, the gallery was primarily run internally and administratively by Mrs. Margaret Wunderlich, a strong, stocky, Germanic woman. Her son Rudolf, a bit older than Larry, devoted himself primarily to his interest in the work of such Western artists as Remington and Russell. He spent a great deal of his time traveling around the United States and away from the gallery.

Larry found himself ensconced in the new office that had been created for him on the third floor of the gallery's premises on East 56th Street. In short order, due to his energy, imagination and sales skills, the gallery began to take on a different character and developed into a major force in the American art market. One pleasant irony was that many of the living artists whom we had collected so enthusiastically over the years began making contact with Larry, and he soon began representing Ben Shahn, Franklin Watkins, Abraham Rattner, Jack Levine, Leonard Baskin and finally the John Marin and Charles E. Burchfield estates. He also reached out and soon added the Walt Kuhn estate, Jose de Creeft, Millard Sheets, Joseph Hirsch, the work of Edward Hopper and other twentieth century artists to the stable of the gallery.

The role of a dealer vis-à-vis living artists is very symbiotic and sensitive, making it a special challenge. A dealer is often a combination of business manager, financial advisor, lay psychiatrist, marriage counselor and friend, in addition to his prime role as a sustainer of creative morale. This complicated amalgam can often lead to warm and strong bonds and occasionally unhappy ruptures, but by and large, Larry has enjoyed many happy artist/dealer relationships over the years.

In addition to the contemporary artists, he also widened

the inventory of eighteenth and nineteenth century works of art by adding major canvases by John Singleton Copley, the Peale family, Frederic E. Church, John Singer Sargent, Maurice Prendergast, John Sloan, Winslow Homer, William Harnett and other significant figures.

Larry's relationship with Ben Shahn was especially close, evolving from his being a passionate collector Shahn's work and an admirer of him as an intellectual and a friend. As his dealer, Larry worked to increase Ben's somewhat faded visibility to the public. Besides exhibitions at Kennedy Galleries, there were two other important events which highlighted Shahn's work.

In March 1970 Larry, with the cooperation of the Tokyo Aoki art gallery, arranged a major Shahn exhibition at the National Museum of Modern Art in Tokyo. The Japanese felt a very special affinity for the calligraphic quality of Shahn's work and the exhibition was popular and successful.

Then in 1971, he spearheaded the formation of a new Ben Shahn Foundation chaired ably by Robert H. Smith, a Washington, D.C., collector. The foundation raised funds to restore the major fresco, *Jersey Homestead*, which Shahn had created in a public school in New Jersey under the WPA program. The town's name was later changed from Jersey Homestead to Roosevelt, and Shahn eventually moved there.

Due to the settling of the building the fresco had been badly damaged and the distinguished fresco restorer, Ottorino Nonformale, of Bologna, Italy, was called in to assess the condition of the work. In a delicate procedure, he and his staff removed the 55 by 11-foot fresco from the wall and shipped it to Italy for restoration. Over a year later, in July 1972 it was returned to Roosevelt and reinstalled there in good condition where it remains today.

Over the years, Kennedy Galleries has given encouragement to younger and lesser known artists such as Carolyn Plochmann, Clarice Smith, George Sorrels and Carol Wald, reflecting Larry's sense of responsibility to pay heed to new talent. Thus, with these new artists, the gallery now reflects a broad range of movements in American art including the Colonial and Federal the Hudson River School, American Impressionism, the Eight, Social Realism and Modernism.

Despite Larry's decided point of view on art, leaning as he does to imaginative realism, he gets pleasure out of the abstraction of a vase or piece of jewelry. He recognizes talent in enamelist and jewelry maker, William Harper. He held two exhibitions of Harper's work at the gallery which showed a wider range of talented artists.

In June 1969, the *American Art Journal* made its debut under the aegis of Kennedy Galleries. Larry's deep commitment to scholarship moved him to create a magazine to fill a much needed void in American art studies. He appointed a distinguished advisory panel of scholars in the field and set out to publish a journal devoted to this discipline.

It was made clear from the outset that this publication would have nothing to do with the merchandising side of Kennedy Galleries and would not reflect works of art in its inventory. It has been a journal which provides a place for the work of serious scholars in American art to be published.

The magazine is now published yearly and has been an enormous scholarly success, attracting subscriptions from all over the United States and throughout the world. Despite this fact, it has continued to be subsidized by Kennedy Galleries through the years and has not been a money-making venture. Larry is undaunted by this subsidy and the *American Art Journal* continues to give him great personal satisfaction as another kind of contribution to the world of American art.

At Larry's instigation in the late 1960s, the first of two publishing ventures was undertaken. Kennedy Galleries and DaCapo Press launched a project for the joint publication of reprints of American art monographs which were important but now unavailable to scholars. They published such volumes as *The Life and Works of Thomas Sully* (first published in 1921), *The Life and Times of Asher Brown Durand* (first published in 1894) and *Robert Feke* which had been produced first in 1930.

An imaginative venture which Larry initiated after Ben Shahn's death in 1969 was to commission William Schuman, the renowned composer, to write a piece of music in memory of Shahn. Larry was fascinated at the thought of how a gifted musician might reflect the talent of a great artist.

Schuman was challenged by this commission and it wasn't too long before he had composed an elegant canticle for orchestra entitled *In Praise of Shahn* which in January 1970, was performed by the New York Philharmonic under the baton of Leonard Bernstein. It was well received and beautifully recorded.

The success of this project prompted Larry to approach composer/conductor Morton Gould to create a composition around the artistic output of Charles E. Burchfield a few years later. With Larry's encouragement the commission was supported by the Charles E. Burchfield Foundation, and in April 1981, the Cleveland Symphony, conducted by Lorin Maazel, performed the work, *Burchfield Gallery*. In December 1983 it was played at Carnegie Hall by the American Symphony with Gould himself conducting.

As Larry had predicted so many times, interest in American art was rising steadily and with it prices for American masterpieces were rising, too. Beginning in 1968, he was quoted in such places as the *New York Times*, the *Wall Street Journal* and other newspapers and periodicals heralding the increased commitment to American art on the part of museums and sophisticated collectors — and, indeed, his predictions came to pass.

In 1968, a Thomas Cole landscape which had sold in 1950 for $2,500 had increased a hundredfold. October 1972 saw a record price for an American painting on auction when *Steelworkers Noontime* by Thomas Anschutz (which had originally been in our private collection) was sold.

As the years passed, Larry purchased for the gallery a painting by Winslow Homer for several million and in November 1985, he represented the National Gallery in Washington, buying for them *Portrait of Rubens Peale with a Geranium Plant* by Rembrandt Peale.

These were only reflections of the attention that American art of the more realistic school was receiving through increased exhibitions, the work of the Archives of American Art, additional scholars entering the field and in no small part to Larry's drive and energy.

He was also cheered by the slow but burgeoning interest of other countries in the kind of art Kennedy Galleries represents. This interest resulted in sales to the British Museum, the National Museum of Sweden and sales to the family of the Shah of Iran through his friend the late Ambassador to the United Nations from Iran, Mehdi Vakil. Also, private collectors from overseas began to collect some of the art from the gallery shows.

Recalling how our personal collecting had begun with modestly priced graphics, Larry turned his attention to this aspect of many artists' work. He wanted to provide fine works of art for collectors of lesser means and give them the opportunity to purchase them.

To this end, Kennedy Graphics was organized in association with the famous and distinguished Paris lithographer, Atelier Mourlot, in the late sixties. Fernand Mourlot was well-known as the lithographer who worked with Picasso and many of the most famous French artists. Jacques Mourlot, his son, opened a branch in downtown New York City and soon many of the painters and sculptors represented by the gallery were making their way downtown to create lithographs. This venture proved successful in every way so that from one could find not only Whistlers, Durers and Rembrandts in the Kennedy Galleries print department but also works by Alexander Calder, Joan Miro, Marc Chagall, Ben Shahn, Jack Levine and others.

This identification with the production of contemporary lithographs led in 1972 and 1976 to the gallery's association with the Olympic Games Committee, in which the gallery represented the distribution and sale of Olympic posters and lithographs in the United States and Canada. A handsome group of works was commissioned by the committee and world renowned artists were called upon to create lithographs celebrating the Olympic games. Artists Hockney, Wesselman, Hundertwasser, Albers, Jacob Lawrence, Marini and Kokoschka were among those who participated in the project.

Unhappily, the great tragedy of the murder of Israeli athletes at the Munich games of 1972 not only cast a pall on the games themselves but also had a negative effect on the sales of the lithographs and posters that year. Not many people wanted prints with the Munich name and logo on them. However, the Montreal games in 1976 went off well and with no untoward incidents, creating a more benign atmosphere for the games and the works of art, as well. This series was made up entirely of American original prints including works by Alex Katz, Alex Neel and Will Barnet.

In 1976 a most important chapter opened in Larry's professional life. Our daughter, Martha, decided to join the gallery on a permanent basis. She had worked part time and intermittently in various departments of the gallery during her school career. Although keenly interested in medieval art, her exposure to and understanding of American art throughout her childhood and young adulthood stood her in good stead. So after graduating from Sarah Lawrence in 1976, she joined forces with her father in the gallery. With her art experience, energy, creativity and loyalty, she brought a whole new dimension to the business and gave Larry a sense of a family future for the business.

So, with the able and loyal vice presidents, Lillian Brenwasser and Joseph Wengler, Kennedy Galleries had an excellent team.

During all of these years, Larry has played a significant role in the creation of major collections, both public and private. A former collector himself, he still maintains that great enthusiasm which has proved so contagious to people like John D. Rockefeller III, Winton M. "Red" Blount, Robert L. McNeil and the European collector, Baron Heinrich H. Thyssen-Bornemisza. All of these outstanding collectors have stimulated him. In placing important works in their collections, he has enjoyed their acquisitions vicariously. They, in turn, have been drawn to his natural enthusiasm and unpretentious way of doing business.

Another of the special pluses of working with outstanding private collectors and museums has been the warm and close personal relationships which have often evolved out of business relationships.

About a year or so after our move to New York City, Larry

began to sell some of our important former paintings to John D. Rockefeller III. We were invited to tea at the Rockefeller apartment on Beekman Place with Rockefeller's advisor, Ted Richardson. As Mr. Rockefeller proudly toured us through his home, I was very admiring of his collection but only commented in the most circumspect way when encountering an old friend from our private collection. As we drew to the end of the tour, Rockefeller looked down at me with a twinkle and said, "Barbara, let's face it, this is simply the Fleischman collection on Beekman Place!"

Larry has prided himself on tracking down lost works of art such as *Ease* by William Harnett, an important painting which had been lost in the fires that followed the San Francisco earthquake in 1901. He was thrilled to be called in on an important cache of Edward Hopper drawings and paintings by a minister in Nyack, New York, who had befriended the Hoppers and to whom Mrs. Hopper had willed the art work.

By a wonderful stroke of luck, Larry procured an important and rare Mississippi River raft painting by George Caleb Bingham which an old lady had willed to her attentive and loving hairdresser nephew. The young man, derided by his sisters who had each been left a modest amount of cash, and having no idea of this painting's value, had strapped it onto the roof of a U-Haul truck to take it some miles away to his apartment, where it reposed under his bed. Fortuitously, he casually showed it to someone whom he met at a neighborhood cocktail party and for whom the faint Bingham signature rang a bell. Shortly thereafter Larry was called in to look at the picture and the rest, as they say, is history. He triumphantly sold this great find to Mr. Rockefeller. Needless to say, the young hairdresser's future was made financially secure!

There have been many such adventures which add a special kind of excitement and drama to the running of a major art gallery. It is never a placid or mundane place in which to work. Larry savors the role of teacher and mentor, particularly when clients new to the American art world cross his threshold. Whether it is Mohammed Ali, who in the 1970s stopped into the gallery to look at American marine paintings, or a couple of young school teachers wanting to study lithographs, Larry is always ready to introduce them to the best of American art.

In 1972, Larry was approached by a young sociologist from the United States Department of Indian Affairs for some advice and guidance. Having learned of Larry's interest in crafts and his role in the art world he asked Larry to accompany him to a remote small town in Alaska called Shishmaref. He reported that there were some artists doing interesting carvings up there, but advice was needed as to how good their works were and how to market them.

Unable to resist such an adventure, Larry accompanied the sociologist to Shishmaref for about a week to examine the output of these natives. He found the trip fascinating and unusual as he met and became acquainted with the people occupying this western tip of Alaska facing the Soviet Union across the Bering Strait. He lived with an Eskimo family during this stay, even going on a fishing trip with them in their boat. Their baby was strapped on the mother's back and all of them, including their visitor, were effectively bundled up against the sub-zero temperatures.

While examining the output of these craftsmen, mostly carvings out of the indigenous Alaskan stones and bones, he was amused to see them storing their finished necklaces, brooches and carved animals stored in ovens and bathtubs which had been provided them by the Federal government. When he asked why they were using these items for storage they explained that the so-called sociologists from the "lower 48" had sent the ovens, tubs and other modern-day appliances to them without realizing that they didn't have running water or electricity.

Larry found the works that they had created interesting and certainly unique to their part of the world and spent some time directing them in a strategy for marketing. All in all, he found it a remarkable experience which gave him many new insights into the particular problems of the Alaskan population and its relationship to Washington, D.C.

In 1975, Kennedy Galleries moved from its location on East 56th Street in a five-story premises to the fifth floor of a relatively new high-rise building at 40 West 57th Street. With the increasing security problems in the city, changing from a street level location seemed a positive move.

In 1977, under Larry's direction, the gallery was brought into the world of technology and became the first gallery to be computerized — giving an invaluable tool to the sales staff. After the inventory was put on computer it was possible, for example, to find paintings by John La Farge of winter subjects only. The computerizing of the gallery has had many important ramifications for more up-to-date management in the last part of the twentieth century.

One of the things that has meant a great deal to Larry in the running of a gallery is the variety and quality of exhibitions which have been mounted over the years and the prize-winning catalogues that have been produced in connection with the exhibitions. The exhibitions have highlighted individual artists, both living and dead, in one-man shows or retrospectives and also exhibitions expressing a particular theme such as "Marin and the City," "Master Prints," "The Work of Elihu Vedder," "American Still Lifes" and "Charles E. Burchfield 1915-1966."

There have been various fund-raising benefits staged at the gallery over the years for different, worthy causes. The Inner City Scholarship Fund (a special pet of our friend, the late Cardinal Cooke), the Skowhegan School of Art and the Joffrey Ballet, among others, have asked to use the gallery for their special occasions and in conjunction with appropriate exhibitions.

In the seventies, a second publishingventure was initiated by the gallery which teamed up with the University of Delaware to form the American Art Journal Series. It featured new writings on the art of Thomas Cole, Arthur Tait, Arthur B. Davies, Edward Hicks, Erastus D. Palmer, J. Alden Weir, John L. Krimmel and others. These enterprises were significant in making volumes available to the academic community.

One of Larry's activities in the art world has been his involvement with the Art Dealers Association of America, where he has served on its board and currently heads its Public Relations Committee. In this capacity he has helped to organize its annual autumn art panels at the Metropolitan Museum of Art and the annual Art Show at the Seventh Regiment Armory each February. Over the years, he has also served on the board of the National Academy of Design and headed the Art Dealers' Division of the United Jewish Appeal.

Another interesting experience was when he served as a member of the Internal Revenue Service's committee for evaluation of works of art donated to public institutions.

For some years he was a trustee of the Skowhegan School of Art in Maine and in 1971 gave them the fund-raising idea of an annual Skowhegan Awards Dinner. In 1972, he commandeered me to organize and chair the first of these dinners at which awards were given to the artists Albers, Nevelson and Tobey, along with and art patron Arthur H. Houghton, Jr. This proved to be a outstanding event, giving great visibility to the school. It has continued to flourish annually raising thousands of dollars for the Skowhegan School.

We funded the National Portrait Gallery's 1982 exhibit, "Charles Wilson Peale and His World," and Larry was awarded the gallery's John Singleton Copley Medal for outstanding service to American art.

During the seventies, it had become more and more apparent that Larry and his partner, Rudy Wunderlich, did not have the same approach, philosophy or style of management, and thus, Larry began to think seriously about a possible change in ownership. After many discussions, it was mutually decided that Larry would buy the other 50 percent of the gallery and that Rudy would retire from Kennedy Galleries. In September 1982, this came to pass, and Kennedy Galleries became completely owned by the Fleischman family.

Since then, the gallery has continued to develop and change to meet the different climate of the nineties with all of its new implications. As an important symbol of these changes, in late August 1994, the gallery moved to a new location in the elegant Crown Building at 730 Fifth Avenue to launch its new strategies with Martha more and more at the helm and Larry eager to evolve a different role and new chapter in his professional life.

CHAPTER 13

Art Theft

ON JULY 9, 1966, A BIZARRE AND DISTRESSING CHAPTER BEGAN AS THE move from Detroit, Michigan, to New York City commenced. We had engaged a New York moving company which specializes in works of art to transfer our worldly things to our new abode at the United Nations Plaza.

We had been assured that this company experienced in moving precious things was exercising the utmost security to protect our furniture, paintings and sculpture. In our new apartment, under my supervision, the crates were brought up to us for unpacking. However, the men wanted to stop the moving process at 6 p.m. despite my protestations, as we were willing to pay extra so that the move could be completed in one day. Nonetheless, they prevailed and seemingly locked up the truck with the remaining crates and returned the following morning to finish the move.

When they claimed that everything had been removed from the truck, I showed them from my list that two crates had not been brought upstairs. They insisted that there were no more crates in the van — the crates containing *Portrait of Joanna Quadacher Bannier* by Gerard TerBorch and *Judgment of Cambyses* painted by Peter Paul Rubens or Jacob Jordaens, were missing.

After much commotion and questioning of the movers, we called in the New York City police who, in turn, called the

Federal Bureau of Investigation because this was an interstate move.

The matter took on an even more unpleasant turn in two ways. First of all, when we stated that the insurance had been purchased by my father's insurance agency who had placed the coverage with the large and well-known company, INA., it had to be swiftly determined that we were in no way involved in the theft. A factor which made this clear was that the paintings had only been insured at their purchase price, not at the current market value, which was considerably more.

The more serious aspect of the investigation unfolded when the Santini Brothers movers who had been engaged by the Henrietta Schum Co. told police that I would not allow them to finish the move on the first day — a complete untruth. The FBI interviewed one of the movers, who was on his day off and apparently untutored in perpetrating this falsehood, who revealed that I had been most insistent that the move be completed that evening and was overruled by the movers.

It is difficult to express our sense of personal invasion and the sinister overtones of this planned crime which engulfed us.

We had gathered some Old Master paintings and drawings over the years because we knew we would be dealing in American art and we could no longer appropriately collect in that field. I recall that during the packing process in our Detroit home, I had naively told the movers to leave all the paintings in the living room for last as they were the most important. Whether or not this figured in the theft of those particular paintings, we'll never know.

The investigation by the FBI, especially agent Thomas McShane, continued relentlessly for 12 years and had many ramifications and convolutions. The strong feeling was that in some way organized crime was involved in this theft. We were told that for a time the paintings were in a Manhattan apartment to which the FBI could not properly gain access. Several years later the paintings were traced to a house on Staten Island, but the law enforcement officers arrived there just after they had been spirited away.

From time to time during the ensuing years, Mr. McShane

would come into the gallery and update Larry on possible leads or breakthroughs in the case, but to us it almost seemed dead in the water. In the meantime, the insurance company had reimbursed us with the proviso that if and when the paintings were recovered, we would return the money to them and they in turn, would return the paintings to us.

In 1978, the case took an even more bizarre turn when McShane, posing as a crooked art dealer, was put in contact with two men purporting to have several valuable paintings for sale. When the two thieves seemed leery of McShane's credentials, the FBI called in a con man named Mel Weinberg, who was working as a government informant, to vouch for McShane, saying he was a crook who could be trusted. Weinberg did so and proceeded with McShane to work out a complicated delivery scheme whereby they would purchase the "hot" paintings for a sheik.

McShane and Weinberg flew by private plane to Stewart Airport in Newburgh, New York, where they picked up one of the thieves. They showed him a suitcase purportedly filled with cash, whereupon he directed them to Kobelt Airport, 10 minutes away in Walkill. The pilot, an FBI agent, radioed for weather conditions — a clue to other FBI agents following secretly in two chase planes as to their final destination. At Walkill, the entourage encountered the second thief, who was standing next to a stolen van containing our paintings, and the men were arrested. Weinberg, who had been convicted of fraud in another case, had offered to help with obtaining the stolen paintings to make a deal for a lighter sentence. He was also working with the FBI undercover in the Abscam investigation (then secret) which involved cons, politicos and bribes. Due to the success of the recovery of the paintings, the FBI cast a wider net in its investigation of Abscam, ultimately finding corruption in the United States Congress.

In order to protect the ongoing Abscam investigation, the charges against the two art thieves were dismissed, but they were re-indicted in September 1979 and were convicted of possession of stolen paintings in 1980. They were sentenced to a maximum of 15 years.

Another unpleasant twist came after the return of the paintings to the insurance company. They tried to exact from us the market value of the paintings, which by that time was considerably more than we had been paid for them after the loss. Larry reminded them heatedly of their written agreement to give us first refusal if they were found at the price we had been paid. He agreed that it was appropriate for us to assume the interest on the money but not a greatly inflated current value.

Their performance, to say the least, was not honorable and they stood fast until Larry threatened to place ads in all the art magazines and journals describing their behavior and stance in this matter. Suddenly, they agreed to our proper terms and the paintings were finally, after 14 years, returned to our possession.

Quite by accident, we discovered that in 1974 an enterprising young journalist named Nicholas Gage had written a book called *Bones of Contention* about two hoods trying to prove themselves to the mob elders. In his tale he describes their theft of two old-master paintings from a young Midwesterner who was moving to New York to become an art dealer. Obviously, with Gage's information about the mob and the FBI, he had based part of his story loosely on our experience.

We have often thought in the years following this amazing adventure that this chapter in Larry's life and career would really make a fascinating television movie. Perhaps someday?

A favorite picture of Larry, 1988

PHOTO BY PETER J. KAPLAN

The Fleischman family
in a typical photographic
portrait of the time, 1931

Larry at the age of five, 1930

1945, United States
Army — somewhere
in France

1948, the first dance
at our wedding

Larry with his young brood, 1953

Franklin Watkins painting the *Family Portrait*, 1955

Archives of American
Art meeting with
Mrs. Edsel Ford,
Vincent Price and
Edgar P. Ricardson,
1955

Speaking to trustees of
the Detroit Institute of Arts
on the study trip to
London, 1966

A U.S.I.A. Advisory meeting, 1958

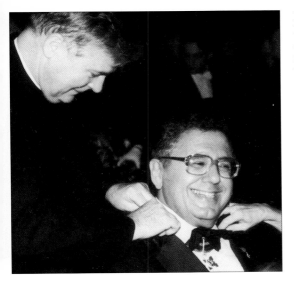

Monsignor
Eugene V. Clark
adjusting Larry's
medal of knighthood,
Vatican, 1978

Jurying an art show
in Minneapolis, 1982

Opening ceremonies for
Fleischman exhibition in
1957 with Ambassador
Beaulac, Buenos Aires

The 1962 Culture Cruise
with Cornelia Otis Skinner
and John Ciardi

First meeting with Mrs. John F. Kennedy's
White House Committee with James
Fosburgh, Stanley Marcus,
Mrs. William Paley, Henry duPont
and others, 1961

Posing on his horse, Drake,
Tombstone, Arizona, 1965

At the Vatican with
Pope Paul VI and
Winton Blount, 1973

The last *J-MAR*, 1979

Travelling back to
antiquity, 1992

Larry with our
ancient marble Tyche
(or city goddess)
overlooking our city,
1989

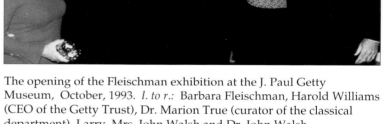

The opening of the Fleischman exhibition at the J. Paul Getty
Museum, October, 1993. *l. to r.:* Barbara Fleischman, Harold Williams
(CEO of the Getty Trust), Dr. Marion True (curator of the classical
department), Larry, Mrs. John Walsh and Dr. John Walsh
(director of the museum) PHOTO COURTESY OF BERLINER STUDIO

Our family, 1993. *l. to r.:* Larry, Rebecca, Martha,
Barbara, Jennifer and Arthur

CHAPTER 14

The Vatican Museum

ON MAY 11, 1971, LARRY RECEIVED A CALL AT THE KENNEDY GALLERIES from the Catholic Archdiocese of New York. He was told that two priests would like to meet with him — but very secretly. Although he was puzzled by this request, he set aside some time and in a couple of hours welcomed two men to his office who would play an amazing role in his life in the years ahead.

As this incredible chapter unfolded, he received the two priests, one a tall, strong-featured American archbishop who could have passed for a Detroit Lions linebacker; the other was a small, bespectacled, bookish Italian monsignor.

Bishop Paul C. Marcinkus did most of the talking as Monsignor Pasquale Macchi's English was limited. He spoke vaguely about a possible exhibition at the Vatican Museum and was probing Larry's thoughts on the subject of the spiritual aspects of contemporary art. The three men spent several hours discussing the essence and the core of art, Larry explaining his feeling that there was spirituality in much that was being created and that one didn't need symbols of madonnas and crucifixions to truly express spirituality.

From the beginning these three men developed a bond and mutual respect. The two clergymen asked Larry to show them examples of what he deemed art with the quality that they were discussing, and he showed them works by Shahn, Baskin and even an oil painting of an Indian dance by John Sloan. They were especially interested in the work of Ben Shahn.

They asked him if he could come to Rome to discuss these matters further. Larry, intrigued by their comments and his curiosity piqued by their vague plans, agreed to stop in Rome at the end of our upcoming trip to Venice in June.

Although my father's sudden death cut short our Italian trip, Larry returned to Italy in July and met with Marcinkus and Macchi. It soon became evident to Larry that these were two extremely important men in the Vatican. He finally learned that Monsignor Macchi was the private secretary to Pope Paul VI and Bishop Marcinkus was the head of the Vatican bank and a close advisor to the Pope.

It amused Larry that at the beginning of his visit, he was virtually ignored at the Excelsior Hotel but once the Vatican car began to pick him up, the attention to him and the service improved noticeably.

He was finally told that the Pope had been strolling through the Vatican after his investiture and commented that, although he saw the spiritual art of the fourteenth, fifteenth, sixteenth and seventeenth centuries, there was no evidence of any art reflecting this quality in the twentieth century. He initiated the idea of setting up a twentieth-century gallery in the Borgia Apartments and wanted to see fine examples of contemporary art.

Monsignor Macchi, a fine writer, critic and intellectual, took up this challenge and, together with Bishop Marcinkus, was secretly building this new museum wing under the Pope's aegis. Some examples had been quietly coming into the Vatican from different parts of the world, but they confided that until they met Larry, they had not met anyone in the United States who shared and understood their view.

At their request, he had brought transparencies of works of art that he thought might interest them, thinking that perhaps they were planning to mount an exhibition.

First they asked him if he would donate the examples which he had shown them to the Vatican Museum. Larry refused, saying that he was unwilling and unable to do that. (He has always had strong feelings that such American art has enough inherent worth that it should not always be given outright.) He said that despite the fact that he is asked to assist many museums and cannot meet all their requests, he would be willing to help the Vatican Museum to procure the works they desired. He suggested that perhaps a committee should be formed to help in this project.

Monsignor Macchi, through the bishop, asked why Larry would choose to help their museum above some others. He responded directly and frankly by saying that since the Vatican Museum has over 4 million visitors a year, he would like all of those visitors to see fine examples of American art as they go through the museum. Macchi told Marcinkus that the honesty of this reply made him trust Larry.

At the end of one of their meetings they asked Larry if he would like to go out to Castelgandolfo the following morning and meet His Holiness. Larry enthusiastically agreed and the audience was arranged. The next morning he was driven out to the Pope's summer residence and was ushered into the pontiff's presence. As he walked the length of the audience room, the Pope arose from his throne and moved towards Larry to greet him. There were several priests in the corner of the room, and after the Pope shook hands with Larry, he signaled for one of the priests to join them, saying that since his English was not excellent, the priest from California would assist him.

The young monsignor conveyed to Larry the Pope's gratitude that Larry was going to help in the work of the Vatican Museum and seemed to know quite a bit about him and his career. Larry was struck by Pope Paul's warmth and extraordinary public relations skills in putting him at ease and piquing his interest in helping the project, which seemed very important to him.

After the obligatory photograph was taken and farewells were said, a greatly impressed Larry left the room and returned to his new friends, Marcinkus and Macchi. They later teased him, saying that apparently Larry was uncharacteristically quiet during the audience!

Back in New York City, Larry was introduced to two more men with whom he was to forge lasting friendships, Cardinal Terence Cooke of the New York diocese and the cardinal's head of communications for the archdiocese, Monsignor Eugene V. Clark. Together they began to organize what would become the Friends of American Art in Religion. In the years ahead, the Friends would be a strong support group for the Vatican Museum, giving works of art, funds and visibility to the museum's collections. The cardinal was chairman of the group and Larry became vice chairman.

Cardinal Cooke was an extraordinary man, kind, compassionate, dedicated to the New York community, with an open and universal approach to all mankind with their differing beliefs.

Monsignor Clark, a handsome, intelligent and affable priest, had solid public relations skills, a wide coterie of interested Catholics at hand and the energy and interest needed to make the committee work. He enlisted the support of Lucy and John McGrath, Mary and Howard Seitz, Patricia and Vincent Murphy and other outstanding members of the Catholic community.

These three men, ably fortified by Bishop Marcinkus and Monsignor Macchi at the Vatican, set out to make the American art section of the new museum a reality.

An unlikely coalition was put together, consisting of devout Catholics who had little knowledge of American art, and some of Larry's collector friends of all faiths who understood the value of having fine examples of American art on permanent view at the Vatican Museum and were fascinated by the project.

In this instance, as in so many of Larry's activities over the years, he has had the faculty for piquing the interest of his friends in his imaginative projects, so he has been something of a cultural Pied Piper. It was no surprise, therefore, to find the Winton Blounts, Baron H. Heinrich Thyssen-Bornemisza, the Robert McNeils, the Joseph Davenports, the William Bernbachs and many others joining in the "Vatican Adventure" regardless of their religious preferences.

Larry soon began to learn that the Vatican, having existed for so many centuries, didn't know the meaning of twentieth century efficiency and swiftness in getting a job done. Being in Rome they mostly adhered to the philosophy of "domani, domani." Notwithstanding that mind set, Larry, with the committee, began to function actively.

In the early days, before the committee was official, the Vatican Museum, through donors, purchased some important paintings and sculpture from Larry, including Ben Shahns, Franklin Watkins, Leonard Baskin, Abraham Rattner, John Sloan, but once the committee began its work, he withdrew from offering them works of art for sale.

Now the challenge was to open the new part of the museum as soon as possible and with the proper fanfare. The Vatican kept delaying the opening until Larry put on so much persuasive pressure that the ceremony was finally scheduled for June 1973. Afterwards it was often said at the Vatican that Larry dragged them into the twentieth century!

On June 21st an excited group of Americans gathered in Rome. Larry and Monsignor Clark, with the approval of Cardinal Cooke and the assistance of Bishop Marcinkus and Vatican Museum officials, had organized a program of unforgettable events in connection with the dedication by Pope Paul VI. Larry had brought his able assistant from Kennedy Galleries, Lillian Brenwasser, to help Gene Clark with the logistics. My role on that visit to the Vatican, and for the years to come, was creating the special dinner menus and planning the very intricate seating.

For five days there was a wonderful mix of events for the group including an archeological tour of Etruscan Tarquinia, a formal dinner as the guests of Prince and Princess Colonna in their palazzo, a reception given by the American ambassador, John Volpe, a tour of the Vatican Library, a special visit to the excavations under the main altar of St. Peter and a final formal dinner.

The highlight, of course, was the opening ceremonies in the Sistine Chapel with the incredible experience of seeing the chapel completely lighted for television. Then, the group proceeded to the Contemporary Art Gallery of the Vatican Museum where the Pope spoke a few words, toured the small collection and gave the group an audience.

Another exciting experience was a special concert in the then-new Nervi audience hall with the Pope in attendance. The

Italian state radio and television orchestra was conducted by Leonard Bernstein and the Harvard Glee Club and the Newark Boy's Choir were brought over from the United States to perform.

An amusing sidelight of the concert occurred when, after the orchestral segment, Bernstein walked down the aisle to be greeted by the Pope. On his return to the podium, the concertmaster wanted to keep the famous maestro's baton for a memento. After a slight tussle, while we in the audience were giggling, Bernstein prevailed and victoriously wrenched his baton out of the concertmaster's grasp.

The small American section of the new museum was high in quality, which was not the case in other sections where a mix of donations from all over the world in some places produced a mishmash of varying quality. Larry always has said that a new museum takes decades to find itself and that everyone has to show patience while a new institution evolves. However, the tiny, jewel-like chapel which had been created entirely by the renowned sculptor, Manzu, was a veritable treasure box. Also, there was a handsome section of Morandi paintings of high quality. In other words, a superb base upon which to build a permanent collection already existed.

This inaugural visit to the Vatican served as a pattern for many other trips to come over the ensuing years, each with a special focus, flavor and cast of characters.

The visit for the dedication of the new museum was so exciting and exhilarating that the group decided to have a reunion in December 1973. The reunion was held in the form of a dinner at the National Portrait Gallery in Washington, with its director, Marvin Sadik, as host. A large gathering of the attendees in Rome made their way to Washington for what turned out for us to be a most special occasion. Cardinal Cooke made some opening remarks and then, in behalf of the group, presented to Larry and me tokens of their appreciation for our efforts in planning and organizing the trip. I was given a beautiful Roman coin of Caracalla, mounted in a Bulgari brooch, and Larry received a handsome Roman medal. It was a very touching evening, and we both treasure our gifts.

The following year, Pope Paul was honored at the annual Skowhegan dinner in New York for his support of American art in the new museum, and Bishop Marcinkus came from the Vatican to accept the award.

In the years following, Larry initiated the idea of having special exhibits and seminars dedicated to various aspects of American art to further excite the interest of visitors to the Vatican and expand their understanding of American art. In 1976, there was a seminar and exhibition of graphics. In 1978, with the help of committee member Nancy McNeil, an exhibition and seminar devoted to American crafts took place. In 1980 John Baur curated an exhibition, "Mirror of Creation," consisting of American landscapes, and in 1983 there was a show of some of the American paintings of Baron H. Heinrich Thyssen-Bornemisza.

The seminars ranged from stimulating to pedantic and boring but there was always something to learn from the various scholars, museum curators, artists, theoreticians and philosophers who spoke to us.

One unexpected speaker was the Pope himself, who flew by helicopter to where we were having our seminar and delivered a serious and thoughtful paper on the spiritual aspects of art. Our friend, Winton Blount, who was the moderator that day, found himself in the unique and enviable position of introducing His Holiness.

On another occasion, where one of the speakers who shall be nameless was droning on and on in a most esoteric fashion on some arcane aspects of culture and art, Blount sat on the dais writing down the names of those who were either dozing or fast asleep — possibly for future blackmail purposes!

Larry's efforts in all of these enterprises were appreciated and recognized in several ways. At our meeting in the summer of 1978, our guest list for the final dinner appeared to be expanding, and Larry asked me why so many cardinals and high Vatican officials seemed to be attending. I couldn't understand either until, at the conclusion of the dinner, Cardinal Cooke, Secretary of State Casaroli and several others came to the microphone and called Larry to join them. On behalf of Pope

Paul they read a declaration whereby the Pope had created Larry a Knight of St. Sylvester, the highest knighthood that can be bestowed without the recipient taking an oath to Christ.

Needless to say, we were all thunderstruck and thrilled, not least of all Larry, who was temporarily stunned into silence. (In October 1986, Pope John Paul II elevated Larry to Commendatore of St. Sylvester, an added honor.) To celebrate this momentous event a group of us repaired to the famous Roman ice cream parlor, Giolitti, where true to Larry's culinary taste, he was toasted with hot fudge sundae creations and towering ice cream sodas!

In 1976, Marymount College in New York City gave an award to Larry for his work at the Vatican Museum, and in October 1978, an honorary degree was bestowed upon him by St. John's University in New York.

Pope Paul VI, of whom Larry had become very fond, died in late 1978 and with him died Larry's plan to have an exhibit of the treasures of the Vatican come to the United States. However, several years into the pontificate of Pope John Paul II the idea resurfaced, and it finally came to fruition in 1983.

We had such fun working with the dedicated staff of the Vatican Museum led by director, Carlo Pietrangeli, the archeologist and scholar and Walter Persegati, the chief administrator and all the bright and interesting clergymen and lay scholars with whom we were thrown into contact. Once, when walking through the Pope's private garden behind the Vatican on our way to a meeting, we looked at each other and said, "What are a couple of American Jews doing frolicking around in the papal gardens?"

One of the most incredible experiences Larry had in connection with Pope John Paul II was during a large papal mass in St. Peter's square when Larry had been asked to present His Holiness with a painting by Joseph Hirsch. During their brief conversational exchange, Larry innocently remarked about the extraordinary creative spirit that fine artists possess whereupon the Pope, his eyes narrowed to slits, turned to Larry insisting that the creative spirit only comes from God!

When Larry continued to reiterate his view the Pope

wheeled around saying, "We must talk more about this!" Larry's view remained unchanged.

All of these experiences in the Vatican enlarged and broadened our lives and deepened our understanding of other religious and moral points of view. We so appreciated the contact with this very different world and what it had done for us that, when we heard that the ancient Roman pine cone outside of the Vatican galleries needed restoration, we offered to help and it was restored beautifully.

After a long illness, Cardinal Cooke died in 1983. He had been courageous and sensitive to the very end. For example, whenever on any occasion we were in attendance and he was giving a benediction, he would never invoke the name of Christ but would speak of the "family of man" and include all religions in his ecumenical blessings.

We all tried to think of a fitting memorial to this wonderful person and finally came up with a perfect idea. The Vatican Museum had no marble conservation laboratory, which made it difficult to take care of the many important marbles in the collection. It was decided to create such a laboratory and name it for Terence Cardinal Cooke. In 1984, it was dedicated with the financial help of the Friends of American Art in Religion and a handsome bronze portrait plaque, created by Leonard Baskin at Larry's request, was installed in the building. In 1985, during a committee visit to the museum Larry and the other hard-working committee members were given a beautiful medal with a portrait of the sculptor Canova, the first head of the Vatican Museum.

During 1987, a new challenge for the committee emerged. In the early part of the century, two brothers named Gugliemi were the possessors of a great Etruscan tomb. One brother died and left his half to the museum. The second brother lived much longer, with the intent of doing the same thing, but in the mid-eighties his child was kidnapped in Rome, and the family was forced to pay an enormous ransom.

This made it impossible for him to donate his half of the tomb, but it became apparent that possibly it could be purchased. Larry and another committee member, Helen

Boehm, organized a group of what they called "angels," who each contributed a like amount towards the purchase of this treasure. It is now reunited in handsome new galleries with the original half.

This was the last major activity on Larry's part for the Vatican Museum. He had become disaffected with the rigidity of the Vatican, especially its decision to prohibit the use of condoms to protect against AIDS. Also, the administration of the committee had changed. There were now other chapters of the Friends going off in different directions, and one chapter in particular was composed of some unpleasant and rigid people who were not too pleased with the inclusion of non-Catholics in this work. Larry backed away from active participation while still retaining his warm friendship with Monsignor Clark and Archbishop Marcinkus.

However, in April 1994, an occasion arose where Clark and the committee insisted upon our attendance. The ceiling and sides of the Sistine Chapel had been successfully restored over the years, and now *The Last Judgment* was finished and to be dedicated. Monsignor Clark's persuasion took the form of reminding Larry that he had been the one who had made so many things possible for the Vatican Museum that at this important milestone he should be there.

We agreed to attend this extraordinary event whereby we had the privilege of viewing *The Last Judgment* completely lighted with only about 20 of us there. It was exhilarating to see this masterpiece brought to such renewed beauty with Michelangelo's heretofore unknown talent as a colorist.

The following morning there was a small mass conducted by a somewhat fragile Pope John Paul II in the Sistine Chapel, where he talked about this great art treasure. Following the mass we few had an audience with the Pope.

That evening a beautiful dinner party was held in our honor, in recognition of the service given to this project over the years, and we were especially touched by the presence of Archbishop Marcinkus who had flown over from Arizona to be part of this event. This was a truly moving evening — a fitting finale to an amazing chapter in Larry's life.

CHAPTER 15

Channel 13 Auctions

Larry's involvement with WNET-Channel 13, New York's public television station, began in 1967 shortly after I had become active at the station.

One evening our friend, Ben Shahn, was being interviewed by Dick Cavett at their studio, and Shahn showed so much enthusiasm for public broadcasting and the quality of programs that Larry had a brainstorm. At that time, the station's logo used an owl as its symbol. Larry asked Ben if he would create a lithograph which would help the station's fundraising. In no time, Shahn came up with not one, but two different designs of owls — each incorporating Channel 13's name in the pattern of the owl's body. When he saw our enthusiasm for both designs, he generously offered to give the station an edition of 100 of each design. They could be used in whatever way Channel 13 deemed appropriate for its purposes.

Channel 13 was duly appreciative and utilized these 200 works of art in a variety of ways to earn money, such as giving a lithograph away with a membership at an advanced level. It was a huge success and generated much-needed funds for the station.

My own participation in Channel 13 activities, which had also begun in 1967, culminated in an enormous project when its president, John Jay Iselin, asked me to organize the first on-air auction for the benefit of the station. Other cities in the Public Broadcasting Network had been doing this for some years, but it was always deemed fraught with too many problems to try in New York City.

So, in the late spring of 1975, an enormous troupe of volunteers joined the staff and me in mounting what seemed tantamount to a consumer products invasion as we began to receive and process gifts of all kinds of items for auction.

I had asked Larry if he wouldn't organize a Art and Auction Day during the week-long auction. He quickly asked Harold Sack, his friend and one of the owners of Israel Sack, Inc., distinguished American furniture dealers, to help him. Between the two of them, they harnessed the tri-state art community. Soon collectors and dealers were being approached to donate works of art, which began to flood in to the station. The art committee was buttressed efficiently by a corps of able volunteers who received the donations, processed them, catalogued them and prepared them for auction.

This general auction was such a roaring success, and repeated so successfully in the following year that Larry came up with a brilliant idea. He conferred with Jay Iselin telling him that he felt that a four-day auction devoted only to art and antiques was more in keeping with the aura of quality that Channel 13 projected. He also felt that they could raise at least as much money in four days as they had in eight days the previous two years. This would also release the channel for more of its regular programming, which would please the viewers.

Jay responded enthusiastically to the concept. In short order Larry and Harold Sack were co-chairmen of what came to be known as The Thirteen Collection for the next four years.

During those years, the lively Art and Antiques Committee (all ardent supporters of Channel 13) scoured New York, New Jersey and Connecticut for donations of attractive paintings, sculptures, watercolors, prints, drawings, furniture, rugs, porcelains, silver and other antique decorative objects. The auction itself was interspersed with interviews with artists, museum directors and scholars and educational spots describing all the museums in the area. Thus, the four-day event also became a learning tool for the community as well as an exciting fund-raising device.

Larry, as one of the on-air auctioneers was put on the spot when scheduled to spotlight a particular work of art. When he saw the horrible painting, which had somehow slipped through the vetting committee, he was almost at a loss for words. It was a poorly drawn oil featuring David Ben-Gurion superimposed on the Israeli flag.

Larry's fellow dealers, the other volunteers and production staff were convulsed with laughter watching him grapple with the problem of how to describe this wretched canvas. His innate honesty fought with his salesmanship but, honesty won out. Through almost clenched teeth he merely gave the work's title, dimensions and a brief description of it. Out of camera range, everyone howled with laughter. Surprisingly, the painting sold fairly well, apparently because of its sentimental subject.

The camaraderie which developed among the committee members, volunteer assistants and Channel 13 production staff was a special bonus during those years. The personal satisfaction that Larry derived out of making an important contribution to the income of Channel 13 gave this chapter in his life enormous pleasure.

CHAPTER 16

J-MAR

TO ESCAPE THE HURLY-BURLY OF THE INTENSE DAILY NEW YORK LIFE, Larry and I decided to try to find a hideaway. Since my parents were spending more time in Florida, we decided in 1969 to look for a pleasant apartment somewhere in the lush Palm Beach area, to use for long weekends and holiday. In a new building called Harbour House on South Ocean Boulevard, we found such a place on the top floor overlooking the Atlantic Ocean. We proceeded to buy it and, in due course, to furnish it.

As we began to enjoy the apartment, Larry would gaze out at the ocean, completely mesmerized by the water as he always had been since his youth near the Detroit River.

One day in early 1972 as we were driving along the winding road of West Palm Beach facing the Inland Waterway, Larry stopped the car at a local marina where they also sold boats. Within a trice we found ourselves the owners of a 17-foot Winner power boat, which we immediately took out for a test ride. It became obvious immediately to my new "admiral" that a 17-foot vessel would not be large enough and heavy enough to cruise over to the Bahamas from Palm Beach, so with great excitement we traded the first Winner for a 28-foot Winner.

When we surprised our children with the new acquisition, we found that they were as thrilled and fascinated with the prospect of "riding the waves" as we were, so we all embarked on our aquatic adventure. Larry engaged a local captain to take care of the boat in our absence and to be in charge of it on our various cruises. We enjoyed local cruising for a brief time, but Larry was truly hooked on boating. It was giving him a marvelous sense of relaxation and fun to learn about this completely different new world — and a new and different world it was indeed!

Larry made it his business to become acquainted with Jack Hargrave, the talented naval architect who resided in the area. It wasn't long before the 28-foot Winner was history, and we were in the midst of picking interior design elements for a 53-foot Hatteras, which was part of a line which Hargrave had designed. We named her *J-MAR* after our granddaughter Jennifer and our children Martha, Arthur and Rebecca.

With the delivery of the handsome Hatteras, the Fleischman family entered the serious world of cruising with a vengeance. With the guidance of Jack Hargrave we engaged Captain Alan Graves, who, although able, turned out over the months ahead to have elements of Captain Bligh in him! This was our first introduction to the breed of men who go to sea and the problems of dealing with them.

We began a series of cruises throughout the Bahamas and southern Florida which were thoroughly enjoyable for us, the family and various friends whom we invited aboard. The Bahamas are so beautiful with their white sandy beaches and handsome foliage. In many cases there were islands where the fish and birds were our only neighbors when we were anchored. Exploring the inhabited islands also proved to be fun. All in all, we had turned into real "boaters."

To become even more proficient and experienced, we enrolled in a Power Squadron course in New York; after a series of lectures, we were given a test. We passed with flying colors and felt much more comfortable in our newly acquired knowledge of boats, how to handle them, rules of the sea and general safety.

Larry's involvement and fascination grew with each cruise and the amusing and amazing adventures we had on these voyages. He developed a keen interest in snorkeling and the beauty to be found under the water and relaxed in the happiest way when on board and planning each itinerary with the captain. It was inevitable that Larry became beguiled with the prospect of working with Hargrave to design and plan a custom boat including all the elements that would make it a fine, seaworthy vessel and a handsome floating home, to boot.

Plans were drawn up, revised, pored over, redrawn and discussed until we found ourselves committed to a striking 66-foot cruiser to be constructed by the well regarded Burger Company in Manitowoc, Wisconsin. So it was that in December 1974, a few of our friends, including Lillian and Donald Brenwasser and Monsignor Eugene V. Clark, bundled themselves up and joined us in Manitowoc to launch our new prize.

The new *J-MAR* was a beauty, with a master stateroom, two guest cabins, crew quarters and a pair of powerful diesel engines. I had lovingly worked on the challenge of the interior design, and everyone seemed pleased at the variety of fabrics with different prints of seashells that I had found to use in the various quarters.

Just before Christmas we returned to Manitowoc with Martha and a school friend, where, amidst low temperatures and five foot drifts of snow, we provisioned the boat and set out down the Mississippi River on our maiden voyage. The Mississippi River adventure was a truly amazing one, requiring extremely skilled navigation, as we majestically made our way from town to town, encountering the fabled Mississippi boat captains, and cruising carefully around the many barges and flat boats that inhabit the river.

Once, while coming through a thick fog, we heard via the radio communications the profane amazement of a captain, saying to all who would listen, "You won't believe it — a white yacht has just come out of the fog!" We certainly were a rare sight to those doughty captains!

As we headed steadily towards our destination of New Orleans, we would anchor at various levees so that we could step out on dry land and explore the local towns. On one occasion, as we climbed up the lonely looking levee on a foggy evening in Hickman, Kentucky. Like a scene out of a Rod Serling *Twilight Zone* mystery, we saw emerging from the swirling fog a parked taxicab with its light on. When we approached the unflappable driver who was reading his newspaper, he told us abashedly that he always parked in that lonely place, waiting for his wife to forward calls to him. Agreeably, he gave us a tour of the town.

Our extraordinary 10-day cruise terminated on New Year's Eve in the New Orleans harbor, and we all termed the first voyage a great adventure.

Since my mother now occupied our former Palm Beach apartment, when we flew south, we would live on the boat which occupied a berth at a nearby marina. As time rolled on, Larry and Jack had many spirited discussions on how to create an even more powerful yacht which could travel longer distances before refueling and would encompass the latest in technology and refinements. Thus is was not too surprising that plans began to emerge for us to examine, peruse and ponder, and soon a new *J-MAR* was born. In 1977, we began making a series of treks (about 19 in all) to Stockton, California, where the new boat was taking shape. We had the thrill of seeing it evolve from its keel to its ultimate completion.

By this time we had Captain Munn, an older and vastly experienced seaman, as part of our new team. Over the years Larry, with his typical commitment to a project which fascinated him, had absorbed this knowledge with study and experience almost like osmosis, so he could bring a lot to the decision making regarding the new vessel. It seemed as if he ultimately knew every rivet in the yacht!

I had the pleasure of working with a talented designer, Edward Bullerjahn, whose specialty was in the interior design of boats. Ed's lively sense of humor combined with Jack's dry and laconic slant on life made working with them a real pleasure for us. It was especially pleasant because, during the course of building *J-MAR*, we four had to spend many hours together.

In December 1977, we took possession of the magnificent new vessel, all 91 feet of her, in the San Francisco harbor. With our four-man crew, the two Stephens brothers, owners of the boat yard, Jack Hargrave, Ed Bullerjahn and the men in charge of all the electronics, we headed down to Newport, California.

On the way we encountered 23-foot waves which caused such pitching and turbulence that I, down in the master stateroom, was virtually levitating on the bunk. Up in the wheel house where all the men were gathered, some with a greenish cast to their faces, they agreed that the ship was indeed meeting this unbelievable test meted out by Mother Nature. *J-MAR* cruised through the storm with flying colors. Larry and I disembarked at Newport, and she continued on down, through the Panama Canal, and up the east coast of the United States to Palm Beach, Florida, where she was berthed.

The next three years saw marvelous cruising for us, our family and friends. The yacht would remain in the Palm Beach area for the winter, and we would chart various trips to Ocean Reef in the Florida Keys and over to the Bahamas. As soon as summer would approach, Captain Munn and the crew would head her north where, on the way, we would meet her in such places as Savannah, Charleston, Annapolis and the New York/Connecticut area.

From there we would head further north, spending time in Newport, Rhode Island, Nantucket, sometimes Martha's Vineyard and on to the coast of Maine. We even headed to Campobello and beyond to St. John and Fredericton, New Brunswick, in Canada.

All of these cruises gave us enormous pleasure, and Larry was indeed the "Admiral of the Ocean Seas" in every way. This vessel carried a small sailboat, a motor boat and all kinds of equipment for a variety of water sports and fun. Our chef, Robes, was truly gifted and, except for his enchantment with kiwi fruit which seemed to appear as a garnish at most meals, provided excellent cuisine.

We sought out places on our cruises where one could shell or, as in Soame Sound, find wonderful stones in the water. One of our most exciting experiences took place while we were heading north in the ocean on the coast of Maine. Suddenly, we found a school of dolphins frolicking in and riding the crest of our boat's wake. As always, we were riveted by their grace and friendliness and spent about 45 minutes observing their playful antics when just as suddenly they disappeared. It was such a precipitate departure that we were puzzled until, all at once, we realized that there was a whale on each side of *J-MAR*.

Their presence had frightened the dolphins away. However, now we had an even rarer and more exciting sight to behold — the whales accompanying us for over 30 minutes in the most benign way, almost as an escort. We raced from starboard to port observing their behavior as they leapt majestically out of the water and even, through our aluminum hull, hearing their sounds and calls. Then, just as suddenly, they, too, swam away leaving us with the memory of a truly exhilarating experience!

We continued to enjoy our adventures cruising, but by 1980, problems began to arise in several areas. The oil supply began to be a problem and our plans to take the yacht to the Mediterranean were shelved due to the increase in anti-American sentiment there and the security risks this entailed. There were also aggravations with the captain and crew. Martha put it succinctly, albeit humorously, by saying, "When dad is returning to the tranquillity of Kennedy Galleries from the tensions of the *J-MAR*, you know that things are out of whack!"

All of these factors caused us to decide to sell the vessel despite all of the wonderful times we had enjoyed on her. That year she was sold to a corporation. We sadly bade her farewell and turned to the next chapter in our vacationing life, which involved purchasing a beautiful apartment at Sloan's Curve in Palm Beach overlooking the ocean.

One of the constructive things about Larry's approach to life is that, once he closes a chapter which he has savored, he turns without regret to his next project. That attitude has governed his whole life. So, while no longer an "admiral," he looks back with great nostalgia on those happy cruising years.

CHAPTER 17

Metropolitan Museum

ONE OF THE GREAT JOYS OF LARRY'S LIFE HAS BEEN HIS ASSOCIATION WITH the great museums of the world as trustee, president, participant in their activities or benefactor. His thoroughly enjoyable identification with the Detroit Institute of Arts and even his position as a national trustee of the Whitney Museum while we lived in Detroit, paved the way for the transfer of this enthusiasm to the New York area when we moved to New York in 1966.

We became passionate visitors to the enormous riches in the great collection of the Metropolitan Museum and began to support the museum in a variety of ways. Thus, in November 1980, Larry was made a Life Member of the museum.

Through his activities at the Vatican Museum and close association with Terence Cardinal Cooke of New York, he pressed the Pope and the Vatican officials to insure that when a collection of treasures from the Vatican Museum was going to be gathered to be exhibited in the United States, that its first venue should be the Metropolitan Museum. This was indeed accomplished and this remarkable exhibition opened in January 1983, to great fanfare and excitement at the Metropolitan.

In October 1981, in connection with a drive for support and new funds that the Metropolitan Museum was mounting, we made the decision to endow the Chair of American Art at the museum which is now known as the Lawrence A. Fleischman Chair of American Art and is occupied by John A. Howat.

In due course Kennedy Galleries provided funds for a Folk

Art gallery at the museum and in November 1983, the Vanderlyn Panorama Room and a gallery named for Martha and Rebecca Fleischman were donated by us to the museum.

These gifts expressed Larry's firm philosophy that if a person has done well in a community, it behooves him to return something back to the community. Over the years in Larry's career at Kennedy Galleries, we had prospered, and now this philosophy was happily being put into effect.

The museum, under the curatorship of the gifted medievalist, Margaret Fraser, had organized an exhibition of early Christian art and was finding it difficult to pry loose from the Vatican Museum several objects which she felt were key to the exhibit. Margaret called Larry who in turn called his friends at the Vatican in Rome. Through his persuasion the works of art were loaned to what was a truly distinguished exhibit.

Through this incident we became friendly with Dr. Fraser, who invited us to the Cloisters to see a large group of superb secular medieval objects which had been in storage there for over 90 years due to lack of exhibition space. She and William Wixom told us that the museum intended to create a space in the main museum if funds could be found to do so.

Larry responded by asking them to give us an idea of the cost of such a venture. When we found that it was possible in our terms, we underwrote what is now the Lawrence A. and Barbara Fleischman Gallery of Late Secular Medieval Art. It is a charming and beautifully arranged jewel of a space leading, appropriately for us, right into the American Wing and was opened to the public in May of 1983.

Earlier, in the late seventies, Larry had been working with John A. Howat at the American Wing and they developed together an idea for creating a support group for the wing on an ongoing basis. With that in mind, Larry suggested inviting people interested in American art to join a group, give an annual stipend and become more conversant with the needs and programs of the American Wing through special activities and events.

Howat, an excellent scholar with a laconic wit, suggested the name of William Cullen Bryant Fellows for the group, thereby honoring one of the important founders of the Metropolitan Museum. Larry asked the sculptor, Leonard Baskin, to create a special medal to be given to the members of the Fellows in recognition of their membership, and Baskin created a handsome bronze medal for that purpose.

Since 1982 the group has grown to about 60 members, and every year there is a special weekend devoted to William Cullen Bryant Fellows activities, including lectures by museum curators, visits to private collections and dinners with guest speakers. Also, during the year there have been tours to outstanding museums or collections in other cities and a variety of interesting events centered around American art.

The funds generated by these memberships have proved to be very key to the work of the American Wing, making possible important publications and often purchases. All in all, the group has proved to be a great asset to the department.

As we became more and more active in the field of the ancient world and therefore closer to the Classical Department at the Metropolitan Museum and its chairman, Dietrich von Bothmer, our fascination with that part of the museum grew.

Once again Larry proposed the idea of a support group, this time for the Classical Department, and Dietrich took to the idea with great enthusiasm. In this way the Philodoros was born. The word philodoros means "fond of giving," which Dietrich felt was particularly apt as a name for this fledgling group, and in 1988, the group began to organize.

The blueprint for this group was similar to that of the William Cullen Bryant Fellows involving an annual membership fee and special activities in connection with the department. In due course, a group of collectors in the field of ancient art became "philodoroi," and their activities began.

Dietrich von Bothmer, a brilliant scholar, especially in the field of Greek vases, was nearing retirement. We, together with our friends, the collectors Shelby White and Leon Levy, decided to honor him and his many years of dedication to the museum by endowing a Classical Art curatorship in his name. In July 1989, this was accomplished so that his distinguished work will be remembered in perpetuity.

In 1991 in connection with the exhibition of the Shelby White/Leon Levy collection of ancient art, we underwrote a seminar which was devoted primarily to objects in their collection on view and other related subjects. Over the years, through associations with other museums and friendships that have developed with their curators, directors and benefactors, we have had the special pleasure of supporting them in a variety of ways.

As each chapter in Larry's life has unfolded, bringing with it these new friendships and associations, he has often commented that "giving back" is particularly meaningful to him and enriches his life.

CHAPTER 18

Antiquities

OUR EARLY ASSOCIATION AND FRIENDSHIP WITH TED RICHARDSON, THE then-director of the Detroit Institute of Arts, stimulated Larry in many ways. Although Richardson was a premier scholar in the field of American art, his interests were broad. It wasn't surprising, therefore, that when we sometimes found ourselves in New York at the same time he would take us around to some of the fascinating characters like Klejman, Komar, Hirsch and Tozzi, who were dealing in ancient art.

We were captivated by some of the beautiful objects that we saw and, in 1950 and 1951, bought several Roman bronzes. Larry's interest in history reached back to the ancient world, so these objects exerted a magical fascination for him.

In fact, we had gathered a few objects, and by the time the museum had an exhibition of ancient art in 1963, they borrowed several of our Egyptian sculptures and my Egypto-Romano bracelet for the occasion.

Despite this keen interest we were still primarily involved in acquiring American works of art. Our financial resources were quite limited even for collecting American paintings and sculpture, so the ancient world had to take a back seat to our first interest.

Even so, when the Hearst sale of Greek vases took place in April 1963, Larry was so tempted by some of the lovely examples on auction that, with the advice of Francis Robinson, then the curator of ancient art at the Detroit museum, we purchased a group of Attic vases. Although our interest in antiquities continued, our life was almost completely enveloped by American art. Our priorities took another turn with Larry's becoming an art dealer in 1966.

Our collecting of American art ceased immediately upon our move to New York, and for a few years Larry was completely preoccupied as co-owner of Kennedy Galleries and its many responsibilities and demands.

In 1982 he was shown a beautiful ancient Greek silver bowl by a dealer and it became our first acquisition of ancient art in almost 20 years. That purchase served as a benign virus in immediately renewing our interest in the field of antiquities. It wasn't long before we had invited Dietrich von Bothmer, chairman of the Classical Department at the Metropolitan Museum and a preeminent authority on Greek vases to see the few ancient works we owned. In his characteristically blunt way he said, "Get rid of the vases. They're not good enough for you."

Since Larry's byword has always been, "There's no substitute for quality," a phrase that has he has invoked all through the years to cover many aspects of life, we heeded Dietrich's advice we began to explore the ancient art market once again with fresh eyes.

Maxwell Anderson, the bright young scholar of Roman art who was then associate curator at the Metropolitan Museum, was introduced to us and became a real catalyst as we reentered this field. He encouraged us by introducing us to dealers, suggesting books to add to our then small library dedicated to the ancient world and in every way fed our renewed interest.

We began to acquire beautiful examples of Greek, Hellenistic, Roman and Etruscan art, leaving the Egyptian world behind, as it is an entire discipline in itself. Over the years we have gathered marvelous bronzes, marbles, terracottas, silver, gold and pottery as our collection has grown and matured.

The special joy of this collection has been that it is wholly a joint venture. In collecting antiquities, as was the case in our American collection, Larry, of course, is the leader, but I have been equally caught up in this adventure. I try to act as a brake sometimes to curb his impetuous enthusiasm and slow down the acquisition program but usually to no avail!

The healthy thing about Larry's attitude toward any collecting has always been that we are merely custodians, not really owners, and that in the long run these amazing objects are "things" and can't possess us and take over our lives. That approach is what eliminates unpleasant obsession and makes it exciting and fun. Our collection has always been open to scholars and others interested in the ancient world.

The most significant ingredient in Larry's collecting that has stood him in such good stead, is his "eye." From the time he began collecting American art, professionals like Ted Richardson have always commented on his natural eye and his unerring taste. As Richardson always said, "You can learn and develop taste by reading and looking, but a natural eye is a gift."

The renewed interest in personal collecting has given Larry enormous challenges and pleasure and a welcome respite from his daily professional work with American art. He savors the opportunity of researching and studying the pieces and seems to get relaxation in installing and lighting them in the vitrines and pedestals they occupy.

Often during the night or in the wee small hours when sleep eludes him, Larry can be found rearranging the sculptures and honing the displays to his satisfaction. I liken this jokingly to a little girl playing with her doll house and rearranging its furniture, an allusion which only makes Larry grin.

We were invited to serve on the Visiting Committee of the Classical Department of the Metropolitan Museum in 1989; and shortly thereafter we joined the Visiting Committee of the Classical Department of the Museum of Fine Arts in Boston. An added pleasure of attending the meetings in Boston is the fact that our son Arthur, who lives in Boston and does volunteer work in the Classical Department, is also on the committee.

In the course of our travels now we meet dealers and scholars from all over the world who have in a variety of ways added to our knowledge with their expertise and learning. The scholars who from time to time visit the collection are most generous in sharing their information, and spending time with them has given a new dimension to our life.

Travel has taken on a special significance as we now organize our trips to visit and study vestiges of the ancient world in Italy, Greece and Turkey and are always planning new itineraries to more remote areas.

In 1988, an important exhibition of great bronzes called "The Gods' Delight: The Human Figure in Classical Bronzes" was organized by Arielle Kozloff and David Gordon Mitten and included three of our bronzes. The exhibition was also shown at the Cleveland Museum, the Los Angeles Museum and the Boston Museum of Fine Arts. A seminar was held in conjunction with the exhibition giving us the opportunity of studying and learning more about this fascinating field.

As the Metropolitan Museum of Art began to show more interest in the field of ancient art, Larry urged them to exhibit the collection of Shelby White and Leon Levy who had been collecting seriously for some years. In September 1990, their exhibit called "Glories of the Past" opened and attracted a good deal of attention in the art community giving more visibility to this aspect of art.

For some time we had been receiving overtures from different museums to exhibit our growing collection. In 1991 we accepted the offer of Marion True, the curator of the Classical Department at the J. Paul Getty Museum in Malibu, to loan our collection to them. Also, Arielle Kozloff, the curator of Ancient Art at the Cleveland Museum, asked to be associated with the exhibit.

Because of our great respect for the scholarship and skills of these women and also our personal affection and friendship, we consented. As our collection had developed we had realized that it called for a catalogue. Now with a planned exhibition, a full-blown catalogue would be a reality and we would be able to share our collection with a wider public.

Over the next three years, with the incredible work of teams of scholars, assistant curators, conservators, a photographer, packing and installation experts, designers, editors, publishers and administrators of special events, the exhibition began to take shape. In October 1994, we traveled to Malibu, California, where we became involved in a series of small dinners, staff receptions and a press breakfast.

On October 12, on a balmy evening under a moonlit sky over the outer peristyle of the J. Paul Getty villa, the exhibition was inaugurated. The exhibition itself was a marvel, beautifully installed, with excellent labels and didactic material — all supplemented by a brilliant catalogue.

Over 200 people — family, friends, scholars, museum directors, trustees and dignitaries — moved through the galleries thrilled and mesmerized by the exhibition which had been so brilliantly conceived and mounted by Curator Marion True and her exceptional staff.

The reception was followed by a charming and gala dinner complete with short speeches by Director John Walsh, Getty Trust President Harold Williams and Larry. The occasion was warm, loving and lively, in the true spirit of a family gathering and an unforgettable experience!

The day after the opening, we hosted a luncheon honoring the Getty staff with many of our out-of-town guests in attendance, too. On the West Terrace of the museum, under sunny skies and overlooking a Tuscan-like landscape, we saluted the staff for their incredible performance and gave special gifts to our curator, Ariel Herrmann, and to the exhibition curators, Marion True and Arielle Kozloff.

That evening, back in the inner peristyle of the museum in which a replica of an ancient stage had been erected, we saw two excellent performances of comedies by Menander and Plautus, directed by Michael Hackett of UCLA, translated by Richard Beacham of the University of Warwick and Michael Walton of the University of Hull. Original music was composed for the occasion by Nathan Birnbaum.

The costumes, proscenium mask and other accouterments had been inspired by the theatrical vases and bronzes in our collection.

We returned to California a few weeks later for Larry to give his lecture on collecting as part of the Getty Museum lecture series. A most touching incident took place while we were revisiting the exhibition galleries.

A school group of 10-year-olds was rehearsing as they were going to be docents on Roman Family Day which was part of the education program of the museum. We were introduced to this group, a true cross-section of the Los Angeles community. It included in addition to American and African-American children, others of Latino, Oriental and Arab background. Although they were new to museum visiting and an exhibition such as ours, when invited to ask us questions, they responded quickly and with intelligent insight. They asked where we keep the collection, how we find the objects, and what we shall eventually do with them. But the most touching question of all was when a lively young boy asked Larry, "Mr. Fleischman, is this about the best thing that has ever happened to you?" Larry nodded and agreed that he thought is was!

After those unforgettably heady and exhilarating days in California we then turned our thoughts ahead to February 12, 1995, when under the directorship of Robert Bergman and the curatorial aegis of Arielle Kozloff of the Cleveland Museum, we shall experience another exciting interpretation of our collection.

CHAPTER 19

British Museum

Larry's relationship with the British Museum began when he occasionally spent time in London as a young G.I. during World War II.

He drifted into the museum and, despite the fact that a good bit of the collection had been stored away for safety reasons, the Edward VII Gallery, a long gallery that showed a melange of the great objects from all sections of the museum, was still intact.

This gallery so fascinated him and remained so vivid in his memory that on our first trip to Europe after our marriage, one of the first things he wanted to share with me in London was the Edward VII Gallery, which was then still unchanged.

Over the years, on the many trips we made to London, we continued to enjoy the treasures of that great international museum as well as the other great picture galleries and museums of the city.

London came to have such a hold on us that in 1985 we bought a small but charming flat adjacent to the Savoy Hotel. That section of the building had housed Savoy business offices, but in 1984 developers carved out 13 modern, air-conditioned flats on those premises. The flat has been a real addition to our lives and serves not only as a home away from home but as a stopping off point when we are headed on trips to other parts of Europe.

It became especially enjoyable for us as we began, in the

126

late 1980s, to become active at the British Museum. We had been introduced to Brian Cook, then the Keeper of the Department of Classical Art, and we were impressed with his extraordinary staff and its level of scholarship and ability.

Before long Brian was struck by Larry's thoughts on creating a support group for the Classical Department, and together they began to plan how to effectuate this idea. Brian, a fine keeper, saw in this kind of small organization a way of obtaining financial help as well as moral support for the department. With this partnership was born the "Caryatids," named after the sculptures which serve as support columns in ancient Greek architecture. Larry has strong feelings that the British Museum is an international museum, a United Nations of art, as it were, and reaches out to people from all over the world.

With great enthusiasm he and Brian began to gather in members of the new group, made up of Americans, British and Europeans, and to plan a program and activities for their edification. Since its inauguration, the Caryatids have had five annual meetings in London, including dinners with special speakers at distinguished clubs and in other surroundings, tours through the current ancient exhibitions, seminars with the staff of the Classical Department and luncheon meetings.

Each year the members of the Caryatids receive specially bound books newly published by the department. The funds generated by their memberships have helped in acquisitions, travel expenses for staff and a variety of extremely useful ways.

In November 1988, Larry and I had the exciting experience of being presented to Her Majesty Queen Elizabeth and Prince Philip at a special dinner at the British Museum and over the years have met the Princess of Wales, Princess Margaret and the Princess Royal. The royal family is called upon frequently to participate in the openings at the museum and their very presence adds lustre to these occasions.

Larry was completely captivated by the blinding beauty and natural charm of the Princess of Wales. She has now taken her place in his small pantheon of treasured ladies with Jeanette MacDonald!

In July 1991, we responded to the need at the museum to

restore the famous Greek Bassae Relief, which had been tucked away in a fashion that didn't encourage visitors and needed to be rearranged according to new thoughts on its proper order. The 101-foot-long marble relief with 23 original segments was part of the internal decoration on a late fifth century B.C. temple dedicated to Apollo. It shows two wars, one between the Greeks and Amazons and the other between the Lapiths and the Centaurs. After the Elgin Marbles, it is considered one of the most important pieces of classical sculpture extant. We were impressed by the work of the conservators and the archeologists as they worked on this project and it gave us real pleasure to play a small part in its restoration.

At the British Museum's Annual Patrons Dinner in May 1992, Larry, as a supporter from overseas, was asked to say a few words expressing what the museum means to him and he spoke most eloquently. Afterwards we were invited to join the director and the Princess Royal as she was shown the newly arranged Bassae Relief.

The year before, when Larry had been presented to the Princess of Wales, then the director of the British Museum, Sir David Wilson, explained to her that we were being very helpful with the Greek frieze, to which the princess in puzzled fashion queried, "The deep freeze?" When it was explained exactly to what Wilson was referring, she laughingly said, "I guess this isn't my night !" Larry found this quite charming.

Since Brian Cook's retirement as Keeper of the Department of Classical Art in 1993, Larry has enthusiastically continued his activities with the Caryatids in concert with the new Keeper, the gifted scholar and able administrator, Dyfri Williams.

In 1993 he began working with the American Friends of the British Museum and in April 1994 was unanimously elected president of the group.

As activities are being planned both in the United States and Great Britain to give this international museum more visibility, a hilarious incident took place in December 1994. A call came in for Larry from the director's office at the British Museum, and a secretary with a clipped, business-like voice asked for Larry's secretary. When she was put through, she inquired if she could find out if Mr. Fleischman was available to attend the Patron's Dinner at the museum on July 11, 1995; a quick answer was needed.

By checking his calendar and asking Larry, it was immediately ascertained that he could indeed attend the function on that date. The British secretary responded with relief, crisply stating, "Oh good — now we can notify Buckingham Palace!" As this was repeated all through the gallery, everyone dissolved in laughter.

Now, as this new chapter is opening for him, he is looking forward to enjoyable and stimulating new adventures.

CHAPTER 20

A Portrait in Words

FORTY-SEVEN YEARS HAVE PASSED SINCE THE EVENTS IN CHAPTER 1 WHEN first I met the subject of this book. Larry Fleischman is 47 years older, but still possessed of the exciting qualities that captivated me in 1947.

It would be a great challenge if I had the talent to put brush to canvas and limn his portrait in all its aspects. However, since I am lacking that special gift, I have tried with mere words to sum up this very special and remarkable man. He is an amalgam of characteristics and contradictions, a shrewd, tough and canny man whose exterior also masks his sensitive, sentimental and intuitive side.

Basically shy, he can appear to be intimidating and detached but when relaxed is winning, charming and often funny. He is a stubborn person who can be volatile, quick-tempered and impatient, but despite firm and seemingly rigid opinions, he has the unexpected gift of a willingness to listen and sometimes surprisingly changes his mind.

Just when you are convinced that you know how he'll react or what his opinion will be on a topic, he will confound you by enunciating a fresh and unpredictable view.

What makes a "natural leader," which assuredly Larry has been all of his life? Besides being creative, he is amazingly persuasive and has an uncanny knack for getting people to work together for whatever exciting project or cause he espouses. He is competitive and likes to be in control.

As a catalyst throughout his years, Larry has so affected the lives of others that many acquaintances, colleagues and friends have found their careers dramatically and unexpectedly changed due to his influence, advice and counsel.

He is everlastingly fascinated by people and is the kind of person who, when placed next to someone new at a dinner party, asks many questions to find out what makes him or her "tick."

He is an intensely loyal friend but, when disappointed or disillusioned by someone, can find it difficult to forgive. It is an interesting commentary on his friendships and relationships throughout the years that, when we were younger, many of our friends were older; now that he has advanced in years, Larry has developed many younger friends. This makes life even more lively.

A collector during his entire life, whether of advertising badges in his childhood or during our marriage beginning with prints and continuing to American art, rare books, Renaissance medals, old masters and then antiquities, he has been impulsive and impetuous, always reaching for the highest quality, sometimes, alas, even overreaching!

This has stimulated him to find new ways of generating funds to feed this passion for collecting. So much so, that in our early years together I insist that I had caught his speculative eye, appraising how much I might bring on the open market! Happily, however, this possibility was apparently abandoned.

Another passion of Larry's is America, which has been enhanced by his love of our country's history. He venerates George Washington, his personal icon, whom he considers one of the greatest leaders who has ever lived. Larry's interest is so deep that he was truly honored in October 1991, when asked to join the prestigious Antiquarian Society of America, an invited membership of historians, scholars and other distinguished Americans which in the past has included such as Thomas Jefferson and Franklin D. Roosevelt.

This has not prevented him from inveighing against the flaws and inequities our government often exhibits, but he is basically an optimist in all things and always harbors hope for improvement and change.

He began as a liberal Democrat who worked hard for the election of Adlai Stevenson in both of his campaigns for the presidency. In recent years, he has moved slowly but surely into the moderate Republican camp, a stance that produces lots of lively discussion and exchanges in our family. Our political and foreign policy discussions ordinarily begin around 6:30 a.m. shortly after delivery of the *New York Times*. After perusing the paper, Larry is at his firmest and most articulate as he presents to me his opinions about the problems of the day.

Larry is very proud of his Jewishness, as essentially a cultural rather than an observant Jew with a strong pantheistic belief. One of the areas in which his Jewishness comes into strong play is the great sense of pride he feels in working with people of different faiths in so many levels of the community. He strongly believes that working together gives others a deeper insight into Jewish people and is extremely constructive in building mutual understanding. Our inclusion in the early sixties as the first Jews to be listed in the exclusive Grosse Pointe Blue Book was evidence of this building of bridges between disparate parts of a community.

Also, when our son Arthur had his Bar Mitzvah in October 1964, the congregation contained many of our Christian friends and colleagues led by Eleanor Ford and Bob Tannahill.

Athur's performance was flawless which cannot be said for the rabbi's. We had informed him that there would be many non-Jews in the temple that evening, the majority of whom had probably never been in a Jewish house of worship before. Misguidedly, he chose as his sermon a paean in praise of President Lyndon B. Johnson!

During the reception which followed the service there was a bit of gnashing of teeth on the part of our conservative friends but mostly laughter. They told us that nothing, however, could have marred the beautiful and moving service.

With the upsurge of feminism it was fascinating to realize that Larry without trumpeting it, is a naturally committed feminist. This is not only exhibited in his constant encouragement of a strong wife, two professional daughters and a granddaughter. Some years ago when discussing the "stable" of artists he represents at the gallery it was illuminating to realize how many of them were women. Larry's comment was, "I never think of them as women, only as good artists."

Larry as a son had a difficult time. In a family situation fraught with tension, neglect and parents who were an ill-suited couple, much of the time leading separate lives, it was not easy to have comfortable relationships with them. However, he cared about them very much and was deeply loyal to them.

His close relationship with my father, with whom he had much in common, provided Larry with a warm champion and supporter.

Although his mother was a troubled woman, Larry was very supportive of her desire and need to carve out a pleasant life for herself. He encouraged her activities, travel with her friends and involvement with our growing family.

It was not as easy to be an energetic and forceful son of a dominating and removed father, but as the years went on with Larry's "declaration of independence" and our move to New York, the relationship mellowed. Also, Larry became proud of how his father dealt with and finally absorbed the blow to his ego that the very traumatic and publicly humiliating loss of the apartment building, the Jeffersonian, created.

A most important factor in the change in the father/son relationship was due in no small part to the senior Fleischman's marriage to a kind and devoted widow, Roberta Platt. Their marriage in 1968 made his last years very contented and happy. She helped him to articulate his pride in Larry more easily, but unhappily, he still retained his stubbornness and unwillingness to listen, which ultimately cost him his life.

Larry had begged him to sell the now modest carpet business, retire and leave what had become a changed and potentially dangerous neighborhood. He adamantly refused. We had flown to Detroit in July 1985 to host a festive 90th birthday party for him. Five days later he and his accountant were murdered during an attempted robbery in broad daylight on the company premises. This tauma has had a profound effect on Larry. At least he was left with the memory of their genial relationship during his father's final years.

Fathering did not come easily to Larry. Being part of his own complicated family situation and a generation of young fathers who, by and large, did not tend to their little ones physically, he was not completely comfortable with the children when they were young.

He was always interested in their well being, trying to give them the best education possible and enriching their lives with family trips and outings. But the pressures, anxieties and uncertainties about his professional life and future and frequent absences made for tension and some detachment.

Also, as parents during the late fifties and sixties, we were caught up in the rebelliousness, problems and revolutionary atmosphere and felt ourselves in a maelstrom with three adolescent children.

Sometimes our judgments and reactions were not the wisest nor made easier with the fact that we are a family of five strong personalities — not one of us a quiet or placid type!

These factors all combined to produce problems and strum and drang in the family during those years. However, we are very lucky. We have emerged from that period, and building on what were inherently strong family bonds, we now enjoy warm and loving relationships, close communication and pleasure and stimulation in each others' company.

Throughout all this time Larry has been generous to his children and a doting grandfather with gifts and support when needed. He loves commissioning and giving gifts to us all whether it is the jewelry of Earl Krentzin, John Paul Miller, Kevin Coates or William Harper, or paintings and ancient sculpture. The only constant is that once he has the gift in hand, he finds it impossible to wait for the proper birthday, anniversary or other occasion and must present it immediately. For a man who never had a birthday party until after his marriage, he particularly enjoys those celebrations.

He is very proud of his children's skill and accomplishments, with Rebecca's work as a senior scientist at the General Motors Research Center near Detroit, Arthur's activities as a photographer and designer and maker of jewelry in Boston, Martha in her position as president of Kennedy Galleries in New

134

York and granddaughter Jennifer's burgeoning career in the media field in Chicago.

As a husband he is warm, loving, generous, a bit romantic and always supportive of my interests and projects — a real partner.

We now joke about his carefully cultivated helplessness around the kitchen and house where, "Barbara, wouldn't you like a cup of tea?" translates to his desire for refreshments and "Barbara, where do you keep the towels?" means that he needs to be furnished with fresh towels. He also is averse to answering the telephone at home even if he is sitting right next to the ringing instrument. My response to these quirks has evolved over the years from exasperation and irritation to accepting bemusement now. I have to face it — he's a character!

One of the contradictions in Larry's makeup is the fact that while possessing the strong drive for collecting works of art, he has no interest in personal possessions except, possibly, for an occasional gadget.

Also, personal vanity is simply not in his character and it has taken careful logistical planning and organization on my part throughout these past years to prevent him from going out with one brown and one black shoe, the wrong slacks with a jacket, or even wearing the same tie several days in a row.

Larry is a day person, an urban, self-styled city boy who is most content at home reading history and biography, watching his Western and classic movie videos and listening to operas, Sousa marches, Edith Piaf and Judy Garland recordings.

He is an indefatigable and enthusiastic traveler, ever curious to see new sights, meet new and interesting people and learn, learn, learn! Larry is known to be a skilled tour guide, and our fellow travelers are always amused that when finishing lunch, for example, he is already asking, "Now where should we have dinner?"

If you ask him about regrets he basically has only two. He wishes that he had become proficient in other languages and that he had developed better writing skills.

Through the years, with all of his experiences and accomplishments, I have watched his sense of self mature until now he seems to know very clearly just who he is. Not surprisingly, he's comfortable with that person.

As I put my verbal paint brush down, I see Larry reaching his august 70th birthday, a bit grayer, a bit more portly, a bit slower of gait. However, his creative juices flow just as before, and he remains irrepressibly curious, enthusiastic and optimistic. He tells me frequently that this is the best and happiest time of his life.

He often says, "There are no endings, only beginnings." He looks forward to the new challenges and chapters in what has already been an incredible life.

FLEISCHMANISMS

Regarding The Art Experience And Art World

There is no substitute for quality.

Art just didn't begin in the 1950s.

Art is for individuals — many can afford prints, drawings, or sketches which are as much works of art as major canvases.

From time to time move your works around so that you don't become too accustomed to looking at them in the same place.

A great dealer can be a teacher.

The day will come when representational American art will hang in famous European museums.

Great collecting is being done all over the United States, not merely in New York City.

One must judge with one's eyes and not one's ears.

A work of art is like a telephone wire between its creator and its viewer.

Reacting to a work of art comes first.

American art may not be greater than that of other countries or cultures, but it deserves to take its place alongside all the others.

Buying art should be for the emotional experience, not speculation.

Art should not be thought of as an obscure mystique.

As collectors we are custodians, not possessors.

TIMELINE

1925 - Feb 14	Born in Detroit, Michigan
1938 - Feb	Bar Mitzva
- Sep	Western Military Academy, Alton, Illinois
1941 - Sep	Purdue University
1943 - Fall	Enlisted in United States Army
1946 -	Returned to Detroit,
	University of Detroit
	Arthur Fleischman Company
1947 - Jun 9	Met Barbara Greenberg
1948 - Dec 18	Married
1949 - Mar 20	First work of art purchased
1950 - Jan 31	Daughter, Rebecca, born
1951 -	National Carpet Design Competition
- Oct 3	Son Arthur born
1952 -	International Carpet Design Competition
	First antiquity and major American painting purchased
1953 - Apr	Michigan Rotary Press organized
- Oct 14	Daughter, Martha, born
1954 -	Art Adventures organized
- Jun	Archives of American Art conceived
1956 -	Trustee, Founders Society, Detroit Institute of Arts
- May	Television station WITI-TV dedicated
- Aug	USIA tour of Fleischman American art collection
1957 - Dec	Second USIA tour of Fleischman American art collection
1961 - Oct	White House Committee on Paintings
1962 - Feb	S. S. *Atlantic* cruise
- Apr	Detroit Arts Commission appointment
1964 - Jan	Historic Tombstone Adventures
1966 - Jun	Dedication of South Wing, Detroit Institute of Arts
- Jul	Moved to New York City
	Co-owner of Kennedy Galleries
1970 - Apr 1	Grandaughter Jennifer born
1971 - May	Vatican Museum
1972 -	First *J-MAR*
1978 -	The Thirteen Collection, Channel 13
1978 - Summer	Knighthood of San Sylvester from Pope Paul VI
1981 -	Metropolitan Museum projects
1982 -	Antiquities collecting renewed
-	Purchase of remaining stock to become sole owner of Kennedy Galleries
1987 -	British Museum projects
1994 - Apr	President, American Friends of British Museum
- Oct 12	"Passion for Antiquities" exhibition at J. Paul Getty Museum, Malibu, California
1995 - Feb 12	"Passion for Antiquities" exhibition at Cleveland Museum of Art

JURIES AND LECTURES

1951 -	Lecture at Detroit Institute of Arts, Detroit Michigan: "The Carpet Story"
1951 -	Appearance on the *Dave Garroway Show*, Chicago, Illinois
1956 - Jan	Lecture at the Kalamazoo Art League, Kalamazoo, Michigan
1956 - Oct	Lecture at the Willistead Art Gallery, Windsor, Ontario
1957 - Jun	Lecture at the Detroit chapter of Brandeis University
1957 - Nov	Juror for *Milwaukee Journal* art show, Milwaukee, Wisconsin
1960 -	Lecture to the Fashion Group of New York City, New York, New York
1962 - Jan	Lecture at the Village Women's Club of Michigan, Detroit, Michigan
1962 - Apr	Juror at the Butler Art Institute exhibition, Youngstown, Ohio
1963 - Mar	Lecture to the American Association of University Women, Detroit, Michigan
1963 -	Lecture at the University of Arizona, Tucson, Arizona: in connection with the John Marin exhibit
1969 -	Speech at the Fine Arts Museum of Peabody College, Nashville, Tennessee: at the dedication of Ben Shahn mural
1969 - Oct	Lecture at the New Jersey State Museum, Trenton, New Jersey: Shahn retrospective
1969 - Nov	Speech at Butler Art Institute, Youngstown, Ohio: on the occasion of the 50th anniversary of the museum
1969 - Nov	Speech at the Detroit Institute of Arts, Detroit, Michigan: to the Associates of the American Wing
1973 - Nov	Lecture to congregation at Shaarey Zedek, Southfield, Michigan: "The Vatican Experience"
1974 - Apr	Lecture at High Museum, Atlanta, Georgia
1974 - Sep	Panel member at the Loeb Center, New York, New York: discussion of artists' rights
1974 - Oct	Lecture at the Midwest Antiques Forum, Dearborn, Michigan
1975 - Nov	Lecture at the Antiquarian Society, Montgomery, Alabama
1976 - Feb	Lecture to congregation at Shaarey Zedek, Southfield, Michigan: "Bicentennial & the Jewish Experience"
1977 - Apr	Lecture at City Athletic Club, New York, New York
1977 - May	Lecture at Milwaukee Art Center, Milwaukee, Wisconsin

1978 - Jan	Lecture at the World Antiques and Fine Arts Market Conference, New York, New York
1978 - Oct	Lecture at the Fine Arts Centre, Greenville, South Carolina
1979 - Mar	Speech at the premiere of ART, Inc., in Montgomery, Alabama
1979 - Apr	Lecture at the New School of Social Research, New York, New York
1979 - Sep	Lecture at Charles H. Macnider Museum, Mason City, Iowa
1980 - Mar	Panel member at the World Art Market Conference, New York, New York
1980 - Apr	Panel member at Personal Investment Strategies Conference at Marymount College, New York, New York
1980 - Nov	Lecture for "Classes for Connoisseurs", Washington, D.C.
1981 - Jan	Lecture at the Antique World Collectors Conference, Palm Beach, Florida: "American Paintings"
1981 - May	Panel Member at Conference on Collection at the Metropolitan Museum of Art, New York, New York: "In Quest of Quality"
1981 - Sep	Panel member at Ben Shahn Symposium, Santa Fe, New Mexico
1982 - May	Lecture at Oklahoma Art Center, Oklahoma City, Oklahoma
1982 - Jul	Juror at West Publishing's "Art & the Law" Exhibition, Minneapolis/St. Paul, Minnesota
1983 - Mar	Lecture at The Jewish Museum, New York, New York
1983 - Apr	Lecture at the Arts Council Gallery, Westport, Connecticut
1984 - Mar	Panel member at the World Art Market Conference, New York, New York
1984 - May	Interview with host Charles Kurault on *CBS Sunday Morning*
1984 - Sep	Speech at Baltimore Museum of Art, Baltimore, Maryland: for the opening of the Thyssen exhibition
1984 - Sep	Panel member on the *Horizon* magazine "Roundtable," New York, New York
1984 - Nov	Lecture at Temple Emanu-El, New York, New York: "Jewish Contributions in Art"
1985 - Apr	Lecture at the University of Delaware, Newark, Delaware
1985 - Apr	Lecture at Panhandle-Plains Historical Society, Amarillo, Texas

1986 - Feb	Lecture at Currier Gallery of Art, Manchester, New Hampshire: "Charles Burchfield"
1986 - May	Juror for regional art show, Owensboro, Kentucky
1986 - Jul	Lecture at Yeshiva University, New York, New York
1986 - Sep	Lecture at Oklahoma Art Center, Oklahoma City, Oklahoma
1987 - Sep	Speech at Butler Art Institute, Youngstown, Ohio: on the occasion of the dedication of new wing
1988 - Oct	Speech at Montgomery Museum of Fine Arts, Montgomery, Alabama: on the occasion of the Blount gift to the museum
1989 - Feb	Lecture at Palmer Museum of Art Symposium at Penn State University, University Park, Pennsylvania
1990 - Feb	Lecture at Museum of the City of New York, New York, New York: "George Washington"
1991 - Apr	Panel member at Ditchley Foundation conference, Ditchley Park, Erstone, Oxfordshire, England
1991 - May	Member of panel sponsored by the Association of Bar of City of New York, New York, New York: "Legal Issues in the Trade of Antiquities"
1993 - May	Lecture at Archives of American Art benefit held at Los Angeles chapter of Archives, Los Angeles, California
1993 - May	Speech to the Board of Trustees of the Archives of American Art at a meeting in the Brooklyn Museum, New York, New York: on the history of the Archives
1993 - Sep	Lecture at the Montgomery Museum of Fine Arts, Montgomery, Alabama: annual lecture sponsored by Blount
1994 - Nov	Lecture at J. Paul Getty Museum, Malibu, California: on collecting antiquities

INDEX